RAILWAY COUNTRY

ACROSS CANADA BY TRAIN

Heritage Fund
Canada
Canada

Canada

RAILWAY COUNTRY

ACROSS CANADA BY TRAIN

PHOTOGRAPHS BY

Dudley Witney

TEXT BY

Brian D. Johnson

FOREWORD BY DON BALL, JR.

W·W·NORTON & COMPANY
New York London

ACKNOWLEDGMENTS

We would like to thank the personnel of VIA Rail, CN Rail, CP Rail, B.C. Rail, the Ontario Northern Railway, CN Hotels, CP Hotels, and the following individuals whose assistance was invaluable: Omer Lavallée, Norman Lowe, Cecil Halsey, Paul Raynor, Deborah Etsten, Lorne Perry, Norman Drake, John Brebner, Al Greenway, Carolyn Burke, Barry Scott, Barry Wall, Gillian Erlick, Mike Dukelow, Roger Witney and Timothy Wilson. And the following publications were especially helpful in researching the text: *Scenic Rail Guide to Central & Atlantic Canada* and *Scenic Rail Guide to Western Canada* by Bill Coo, *The Last Spike* by Pierre Berton and *Van Horne's Road* by Omer Lavallée.

Dudley Witney and Brian D. Johnson

PHOTO CREDITS

All photographs are by Dudley Witney, with the exception of the following: *Archives of the Canadian Rockies/Peter and Catharine Whyte Foundation:* page 132; *Canadian Pacific Archives:* pages 93, 95, 168, 197 right; *Glenbow Archives, Calgary, Alberta:* page 167; *Metropolitan Toronto Library:* pages 57, 89, 197 left, 199; *Notman Photographic Archives/McCord Museum:* pages 60, 61, 62, 63, 96, 131, 134, 161, 164, 165, 166 top, 196; *Provincial Archives of Newfoundland and Labrador:* pages 17, 20, 23, 198; *Public Archives Canada:* pages 18 (C 54484), 22 (PA 41121), 92 (PA 69801), 94 (C 68714), 129 (PA 38495), 133 (PA 9455) 162 (PA 11250), 166 bottom (C 9683).

Page 1: A maintenance worker on a speeder in the yards of Victoria, British Columbia. The motorized descendant of the handcar, the speeder is a one-cylinder "putt-putt" that ranks as the railway's least sophisticated form of locomotion.

Pages 2 and 3: A grain train on the Canadian National line on the south shore of the Fraser River, British Columbia. Across the water are the Coast Mountains.

Page 4: The Canadian heading out of the rising sun in western Ontario's Lake of the Woods country. For 382 miles between Thunder Bay, Ontario, and Molson, Manitoba, the line is double-tracked to handle the heavy volume of grain traffic.

Page 5: A six-wheel truck on the Assiniboine, an executive business car that was built for the Canadian Pacific Railway in 1929 and is still used by company personnel today.

Page 7: An engineer reporting for work on the Ontario Northland Railway carries a battered lunch pail — one item of railway gear that is immune to modernization.

First American edition 1985

ISBN 0-393-02234-X

W. W. Norton & Company, Inc.
500 Fifth Avenue, New York, NY 10110

W.W. Norton & Company, Ltd.
37 Great Russell Street, London WCIB 3NU

Design by Don Fernley
Typesetting by Compeer Typographic Services
Printing and Binding by Amilcare Pizzi, S.p.A.

Printed in Italy

1 2 3 4 5 6 7 8 9 0

CONTENTS

FOREWORD BY DON BALL, JR. 8

INTRODUCTION 10

THE ATLANTIC PROVINCES 16

THE ST. LAWRENCE RIVER VALLEY 56

THE GREAT LAKES 88

THE PRAIRIES 128

THE MOUNTAINS 160

A GUIDE TO CANADA'S RAILWAYS 195

FOREWORD

I came close to comprehending the tremendous size of Canada when I was walking through Canadian Pacific's Windsor Station in Montreal early one Friday afternoon some years ago to take a few pictures of the stone Romanesque station. I had spent the entire week inside, at a convention in Montreal, and felt a little railroad photography was well-deserved before I had to head for Dorval Airport and my flight back to New York.

Upon entering the waiting room, I heard the announcement that Canadian Pacific's (now VIA Rail's) train No. 140 to Sherbrooke was boarding, on the line that heads east almost 500 miles to Saint John. I headed out on the platform to take a look at the wine-red train and to photograph it departing the station. As usual, I was very impressed with the cleanliness of the train, and I felt the sense of pride the Canadian Pacific and Canadians had for their trains. Over on the next track was the gleaming, stainless steel streamlined Canadian — certainly the glamour train of the Canadian Pacific. I had seen the Canadian before, but I had never taken the time to get a real close-up look at her. As I walked her full length, I was once again struck by the beautiful condition of the silver and wine-red striped cars that made up this pretty train. I noted the dining car, "Louise," with its Canadian Pacific beaver logos in bas-relief at each end of the car. I longed to be on board the sleeper, "Château La Salle," in one of the drawing rooms for a night's sleep over the rails. And at the rear, was the domed observation car, "Algonquin Park." I asked the porter if I could take a quick look inside and I promptly received welcomed permission to "come aboard." What made the biggest impression on me were the original murals painted by members of the Royal Canadian Academy of Arts that adorned the 1955 Budd-built car. Everything was imbued with the pride of a nation!

But wait a minute! Did I say a "night's sleep" on the train? The Canadian is certainly a fast, modern trans-continental streamliner, but how far would I get in one afternoon and a night? Sure, I was used to getting "from here to there" over-

A passenger locomotive encrusted with snow after crossing the Prairies in December. Canada's seasonal extremes are hard on its aging rail-passenger fleet. It is the only country in the industrialized world that still uses steam-heated cars.

A stack of used rails in Midway, British Columbia. The country's rail system has receded considerably since the boom years of the early twentieth century. The railways are still tearing up spur lines that have outlived their usefulness.

night on most long-haul trains, but I had never really comprehended how long I would ride on a transcontinental train. I picked up a timetable and started to grasp the awesome size of Canada. "Your attention, please; *votre attention, s'il vous plaît.* Train number one, the Canadian . . ." Closer scrutiny of the timetable showed me that I would be in Port Arthur in just about twenty-four hours. In *another* twenty-four hours, I would be crossing that vast ocean of wheat, nearing Calgary, arriving at 2:45 P.M., Central Time, Sunday afternoon. Finally, the Canadian would arrive in Vancouver on *Monday* morning, 11:20 A.M. Pacific Time — 2:20 *my* time! It would cross five huge and diverse provinces and include the spectacular climb over — and through — the Rockies.

When I think of the fact that only twenty-five million people live in this country that is second in size to the Soviet Union, the implications are enormous. We have to remember that Canada is yet a young nation; that just a scant one hundred years ago, Parliament signed the contract for the construction of the Canadian Pacific to link both coasts. The CPR was built through wilderness at an unprecedented rate of up to three and a half miles of completed track a day. The line was finished on November 7, 1885, with railway visionary and backer Donald Smith driving the golden spike into the heart of the Rockies at Craigellachie, British Columbia. Seven months after the transcontinental line was open, the Pacific Express made the first pioneering journey west from Montreal to Port Moody (twelve miles east of Vancouver) with twelve mahogany cars, arriving just fifteen minutes late. The trip took five and a half days — far better than the six months required overland.

Now, it is time to close the typewriter, get on board and leave the rest to the railway, to Brian Johnson's pen, and Dudley Witney's camera. Time to sit back, relax and drink in some of the splendor of Canada. As we travel together, let us listen to the sounds of the railway — and Canada. Let us not forget that Canadians hear in the locomotive whistle the frontier music of their forefathers, and the shout of a growing nation.

Don Ball, Jr.

INTRODUCTION

Above: The Canadian crossing the Red River into Winnipeg, Manitoba.

Left: Looking west along the Bow Valley between Banff and Lake Louise in Alberta.

A train is a camera continuously rolling with irretrievable footage. The landscape moves past the window like a motion picture. And for the passenger traveling across Canada, the movie is an epic one, with images that unfold over vast distances.

Traversing the country from coast to coast, without stopovers or diversions, takes a full week by train. You can make the trip by car, but it is more like watching television: the road itself becomes a numbing distraction, insulating the field of vision, and too many interruptions mar the continuity. The train, which threads its way across the land with a constant momentum, is the only medium that can authentically convey the scale of Canada.

The proportions are extraordinary. With just twenty-five million inhabitants scattered over a country second in size only to the Soviet Union, Canada has more railway per capita than any nation in the world. There are about fifty thousand miles of track within its frontiers, enough to go twice around the circumference of the planet. Railways also play a tangible role in defining Canada. They staple together its disparate regions and cut across its most dramatic landscapes. They transport the natural resources that are the foundation of its economy. And historically they have served as physical proof of the audacious premise that such a small nation could exert sovereignty over such an immense territory.

It is often said that without the railway Canada would not exist. Both were conceived in the same breath of history — the British North America Act, by which the country was founded in 1867 as the union of the Province of Canada (Quebec and Ontario), New Brunswick and Nova Scotia. The latter two provinces entered Confederation only after the new government promised to build a railway linking them to the rest of the country. Prince Edward Island joined in 1873 because it had run out of money for its own railway project. And British Columbia's entry in 1871 hinged on a promise that a line would be driven to the Pacific coast. That first transcontinental road, laid by the Canadian Pacific Railway with record-breaking speed

more than a century ago, opened the west to its first wave of immigration. It created a string of cities and towns across virgin territory and led to the creation of Saskatchewan and Alberta as provinces within Confederation.

The CPR line still serves as the main axis of civilization in the west. Its route was a controversial choice. Rejecting proposals for a more northern route, the CPR decided to take the most direct path possible, although it meant blasting through the granite ramparts of Lake Superior's shoreline and finding an opening through the Rocky Mountains where none was supposed to exist. The CPR also rejected the easy option of a southern detour around the Great Lakes through the United States, which would have lengthened the line and violated its all-Canadian integrity.

The prime movers behind the project were the CPR's president, George Stephen, and its iron-willed general manager, William Van Horne. A financial wizard, Stephen almost mortgaged his sanity trying to raise the enormous funds required to keep

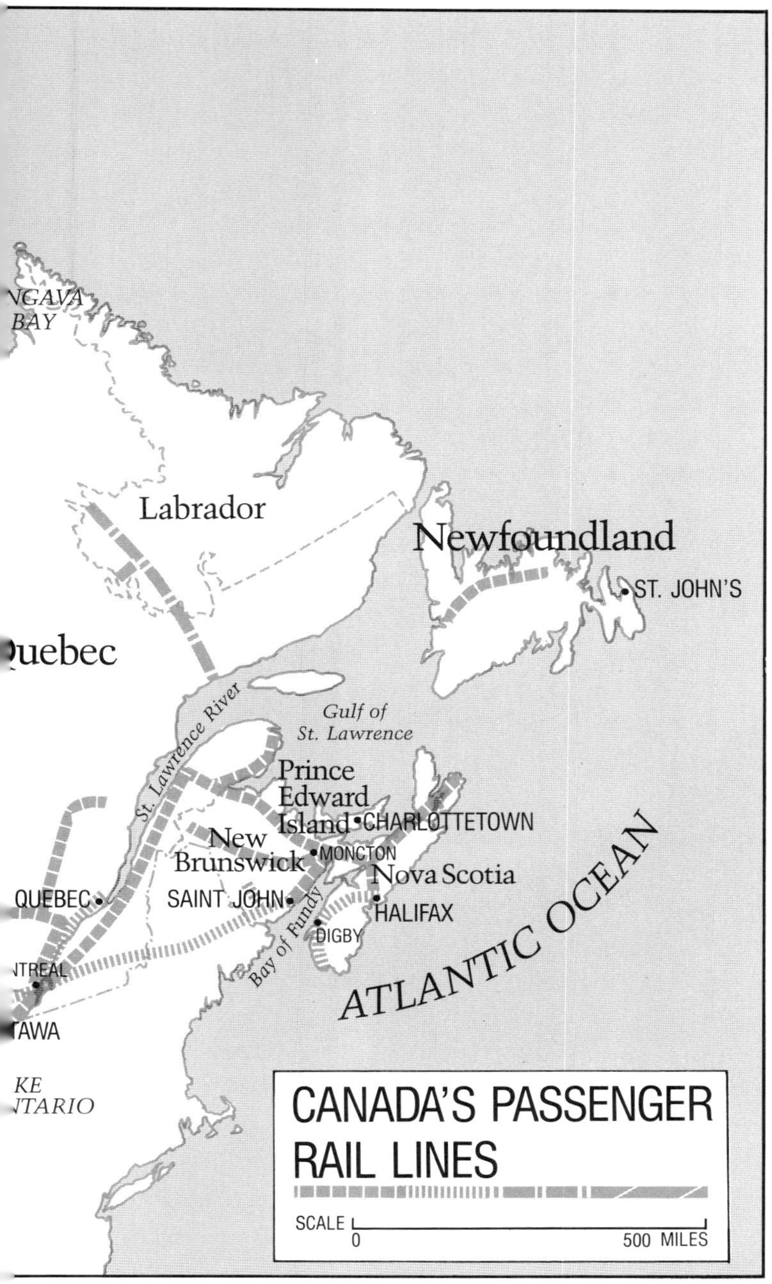

the railway solvent. Van Horne, a renaissance Yankee whose hobbies ranged from rose gardening to all-night gambling, marshaled the army that charted the route and laid the track over some of the most inhospitable terrain imaginable. With men, horses and dynamite providing all the muscle, the line was begun in 1881 and completed in 1885. The feat was unparalleled in engineering history.

In the wake of the CPR's triumph, driving transcontinental lines across the wilderness became a national obsession. By 1915, there were two more railways spanning the country: the Canadian Northern and the Grand Trunk Pacific in the west, linked with the National Transcontinental in the east. By the end of the First World War, all three were on the brink of bankruptcy, as were most other lines except the CPR. In 1919, the federal government created the Canadian National Railways to absorb 221 debt-ridden railways, including the new transcontinental lines. The publicly owned CNR and the privately owned CPR have since become the yin and yang of Canadian transportation, rival empires that have expanded into hotels, shipping, trucking, communications and real estate.

For many years, CN and CP competed for the favor of the rail passenger, and both ran trains from Montreal to Vancouver. CN's Super-continental took a northern route through Edmonton and Jasper, while the Canadian plied the CP route through Calgary and Banff. Passenger traffic, especially over such great distances, was consistently unprofitable, and in 1977 CN and CP gladly surrendered their passenger mandates to a new government corporation, VIA Rail, which terminated a number of trains, including the Super-continental. Early in 1985, the government promised to reinstate six of the canceled runs and replace aging equipment. The fate of passenger travel, which requires heavy subsidies, remains a perennial source of national controversy: the railway that was born out of political turmoil has yet to escape it.

Crossing Canada by train is not as popular as it once was. The Canadian is heavily booked by tourists during the summer months, but airlines have replaced railways as the primary mode of long-distance travel. People who take extended train trips are usually those who consider flying too expensive or too dangerous, or those who quite simply have an undying affection for trains. Although the golden age of passenger travel is over, and veteran travelers complain about the decline in service, the Canadian still offers a classic ride. Covering some three thousand miles in four and a half days, it travels a greater distance than any passenger train in the world with the exception of the Soviet Trans-Siberian Express. It certainly offers the longest dome-car ride anywhere.

The excursion documented in the following pages spans Canada not just from coast to coast, but from a railway on an island in the Atlantic to a railway on an island in the Pacific. It starts on a narrow-gauge line by the shores of Newfoundland and ends on Vancouver Island's Malahat Dayliner. The itinerary is by no means all-inclusive. Except for a few irresistible digressions —such as a jaunt around Quebec's Gaspé Peninsula and a ride on the British Columbia Railway—it takes a direct route across

the country. Geographically, the journey covers a narrow slice of Canada, whose latitudes extend from the high Arctic to a point parallel with Rome, but demographically it cuts through the heart of the nation. Ninety percent of the Canadian people live within two hundred miles of the American border, and the main east-west rail corridors form the center of gravity for urban settlement. With the society arrayed in such a linear fashion, a single transcontinental journey takes a traveler through nearly all the major cities. Yet, what invariably leaves the strongest visual impression are the vast spaces in between.

Because North America's main geological features (such as the Rockies) run from north to south, a trip from east to west takes in an enormous variety of terrain. The railway does not pass over the land so much as through it. Clinging to shorelines, winding along gorges, burrowing under mountains, it has carved a permanent niche in the landscape. And this surgically implanted steel artery provides the most obvious evidence of the fact that there is more to the landscape than scenery: natural resources move the Canadian economy, and the railway moves the resources. Grain, lumber, pulpwood, coal, potash, sulphur, copper, nickel, iron, petrochemicals — they are the priority travelers of Canada's rail system. The only motive that has ever justified the insanity of threading ribbons of steel through miles of solid rock is the money to be made from freight. Passenger traffic has survived as a pleasant by-product.

The railway delivers both the scenery and the resources extracted from it. For the passenger, the most consistent motif sliding past the window is the endless repetition of evergreens,

A burnt-out brake shoe lying on roadbed ballast in Newfoundland. Brakes take a beating on the island's narrow-gauge railway, which is famous for its severe grades and curves.

Platform exit in the CPR's old Winnipeg station. All passenger traffic now flows through the CNR station. Built in 1904, the CPR station is a grandiose relic of a golden age when the horizons of railway expansion seemed unlimited.

a reminder that the country's largest single source of employment is the harvesting of trees. On the treeless Prairies, as the passenger is surrounded by a sea of wheat for twenty-four hours, one hundred fifty hopper cars of grain may flash by the window. On a grade through a mountain pass, a mile-long coal train waits on a siding.

The advanced technology of the railway's operation is, in fact, most evident in the way it handles coal, that vintage fuel of the early Industrial Revolution. British Columbian coal is carried by hundred-car unit trains that are never uncoupled and never stop to load or unload. They travel around a wide loop of track at the terminal, where they are automatically filled with coal and coated with a rubberizing spray to prevent dust from blackening the scenery. Then, at a Pacific port, they pass through another loop, where each car dumps its load by means of a rotating coupler. Such a mechanism may seem more like an enormous conveyor belt than a train, but such is the scale of the Canadian rail system.

The photographs that follow — images of trains and from trains — are a series of moments from a moving picture that does not slow down or stop for the camera. Except for photos taken in stations and yards, the shutter clicked in concert with the movement of the train. For each frame that wound past the lens, there was a corresponding measure of track. The writer traced the same route as the photographer. His narrative serves partially as a guide and a history, and partially as a chronicle of places he passed and people he met. There is always a random element to such encounters, as there is to the most casual glance out the window: that is the magic of train travel. The schedule, the route and the rhythms of the trip are all taken care of — leaving the mind free to wander.

THE ATLANTIC PROVINCES

Above: A wooden trestle over the Codroy River in western Newfoundland (*c.* 1900).

Left: Fenced-off lawns form a tidy oasis against the rugged expanse of Newfoundland's coastal terrain.

The journey starts on the island they call the Rock. Lying like a giant anchor off the country's Atlantic coast, the island of Newfoundland is where Canada begins and ends. Its desolate shores were the first to feel the white man's footsteps, and it was the first overseas colony in the British Empire. It was also the last province to join Canadian Confederation, and it is one of the last places on earth where one should attempt to catch a train.

Newfoundland has a railway unlike any other in the country. Built in halting stages from 1881 to 1898, it is composed exclusively of narrow-gauge track only 3 feet, 6 inches wide. (Standard gauge measures 4 feet, 8½ inches.) Spanning a rugged, sparsely populated terrain of Precambrian rock bristling with modest evergreens, the line was never expected to generate much revenue. In marked contrast to the engineering extravagances of the mainland lines, everything about the Newfoundland railway, from its narrow gauge to its tangled route, reflects the frugality of its construction. Snaking helter-skelter across the island's rolling contours, the track goes over and around hills and valleys rather than through them. There is not a single tunnel on the entire line; grades are steeper than anything to be found in the Rocky Mountains, and the sharpest curves occur on the steepest grades.

Passenger travel is now virtually extinct on Newfoundland's railway. The legendary Newfie "Bullet," perhaps the slowest train in the world to earn such a nickname, completed its last coast-to-coast run in 1969. In good weather, the Bullet would take twenty-four hours to wend its way across the 548 miles between St. John's and Port aux Basques, and the weather was not always good. Because storms had been known to blow cars off the rails, the railway employed a human wind gauge who used his nose to judge if it was safe for the train to pass along gusty stretches of track. If the verdict was negative, the crew would chain the train to the track until the storm died down. During winter months, on a plateau in the northern interior known as the Barrens, huge snowdrifts often stranded the Bullet for days on end. In 1949, a train was marooned there for more than two weeks.

The only passenger service left in Newfoundland is on a 138-mile section between Bishop's Falls and Cornerbrook, which includes a stretch of the Barrens where there are still no roads. To call it a passenger service is generous. Basically, it is a freight train to which one or two coaches are tacked for hunters who have no other way of reaching their cabins in the wilderness.

People do not come all the way to Newfoundland just to take a train. Still, there seemed to be no more appropriate place to start a trans-Canadian trek than the island capital of St. John's, the oldest and most easterly city in North America.

Although nothing but freight moves by rail in and out of St. John's, a new railway hotel, built by CN, overlooks the elephant-gray rocks that enclose the harbor. At the other end of town, next to the dockside freight yards, is the railway station, a squat building made of granite cut from a quarry in the Barrens. It now serves as a bus terminal. I took a northbound bus up a coast road that runs close to the old Bullet route, passing through hamlets with names like Goobies, Gambo and Come-by-Chance. After seven hours we reached the village of Bishop's Falls. From there, a mixed passenger-freight train was due to depart at 9:30 the next morning. It did not appear until 11:45, and then a slow dance of shunting and coupling delayed the departure another two hours.

A brutal wind was kicking up whitecaps on the Exploits River when we finally pulled out of Bishop's Falls. In the west, low-slung clouds were sealing gaps in the sky. I rode in the locomotive with the engineer and the brakeman. It was a boxy orange diesel with the cab at the back. Behind us were two locomotives, run by remote control, and eighty-three freight cars, with an old gray passenger coach and a caboose coupled on the end. The coach, heated by an oil stove with a chimney, was empty and would remain so for the whole trip. The engineer was worried that three twelve-hundred-horsepower locomotives would not be strong enough to pull the load over the Barrens. The dispatcher assured him there had been no mistake.

"Okay," sighed the engineer, "it's your train." There was a raucous crossfire of radio voices and a shriek of compressed air as the brakes were tested. When the engineer backed up, he stuck his head out the window as if he were parking a car, although the end of the train was almost a mile away.

Once we were well under way, the engineer and brakeman unfolded foil-wrapped lunches as if by some cue and ate in bored silence. Suddenly a black bear appeared up ahead. It lumbered slowly onto the track and down the embankment. The crew perked up. They were accustomed to moose and caribou, which were so numerous there were occasional collisions, but bears were an uncommon sight.

As we headed west, the terrain became more austere, and the sky turned gray with clouds smudged across clouds, like a watercolor made ragged by too many brush strokes. We began the slow climb up the Barrens plateau. In the days of the Bullet, it is said, passengers could get out along this stretch and pick a cup of partridge berries before the rear of the train caught up with them. We had almost completed the ascent when a yellow light, indicating that the wheels were slipping, began flashing

Working on a rock cut along the Saint John Valley Railway near Woodstock, New Brunswick, in 1913.

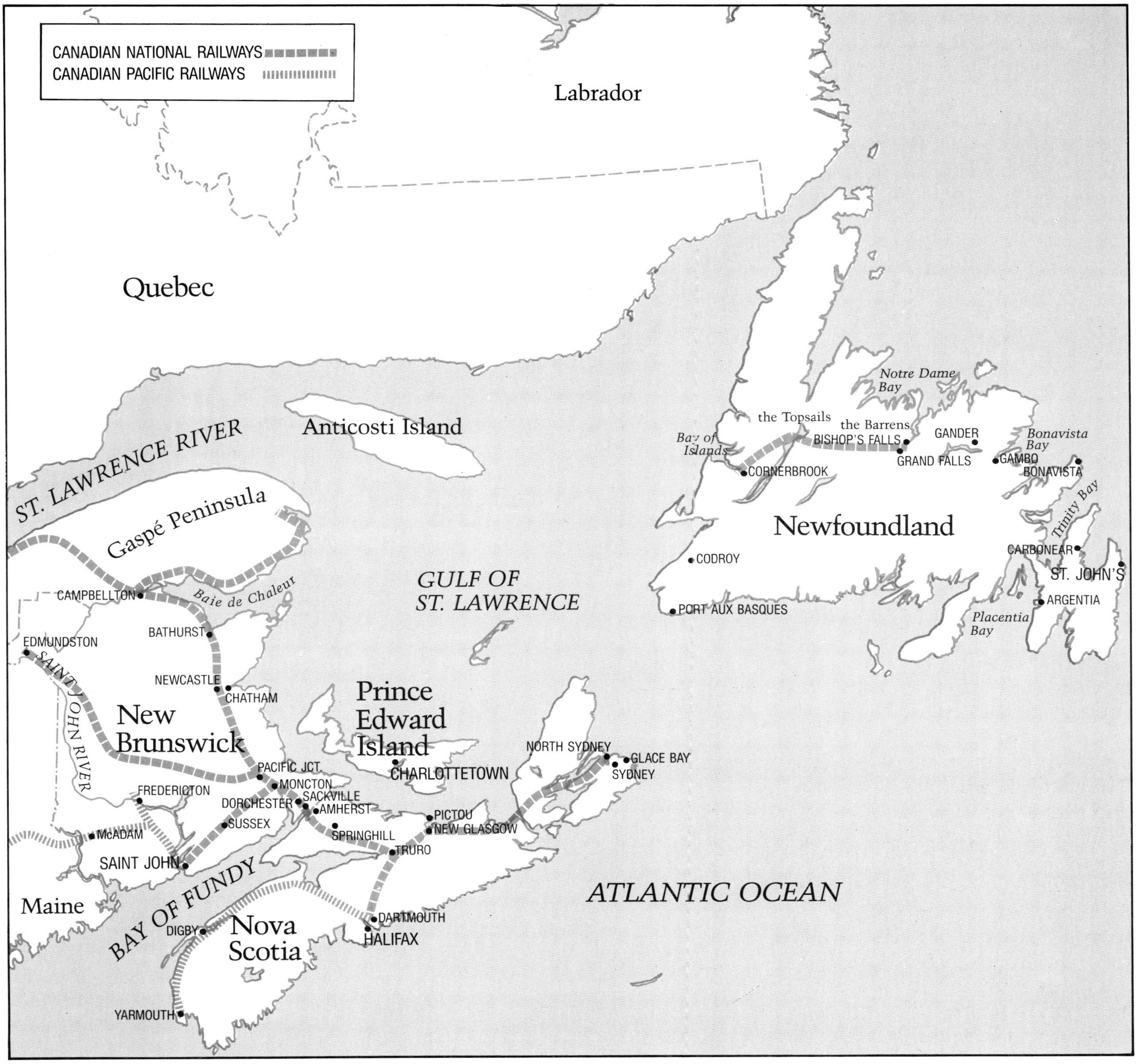

at the controls. Then the engine behind us fell silent. The brakeman walked back to find a tripped circuit breaker, which he flipped back on, and we resumed our crawl up the grade. A few minutes later, the second engine went dead again. With a sigh, the brakeman walked back and reopened the fuse box labeled DANGER 600 VOLTS. He did not seem alarmed by, or even interested in, the fact that white smoke poured out of it. He just ambled over to the door and opened it to let the night air cool off whatever was on fire.

The second engine was now permanently out of commission, and the engineer had the unenviable task of moving eighty-three freight cars from a standstill on a heavy grade with only two locomotives.

"Let's wait till she pumps up good, then give her a little try and see what happens," he said. He gently applied the throttle. Again the yellow light flashed to show the wheels were slipping. He blasted a jet of sand on the track, then pumped the throttle and tapped out prayers on the brass lever of the air brake, which looked and sounded not unlike an oversized cappuccino machine.

The train crept forward a few inches, a few feet . . . and stopped. It seemed to be on the verge of sliding back when, with an exertion that seemed more mental than physical ("I think I can, I think I can"), it lurched forward and kept going. In five minutes, we had reached the top of the plateau, marked by a small sign: SUMMIT 1,566 FEET. It was almost dark. But the silhouettes of three isolated peaks could be seen protruding from the plateau. Aligned like the spars of a three-masted sailing ship, they are known as the Topsails — the Main, Mizzen and Gaf Topsails. Around them is a flat marshland dotted with stunted spruce. The engineer said he had often been stranded here in winter in blizzards so intense that the crew was confined to the locomotive for days. They ate canned foods and kept the diesel constantly idling to stay warm. In the steam

The Bay of Islands on the west coast of Newfoundland (*c.* 1895).

era, the men had to set out on snowshoes to look for wood when supplies ran low.

We headed down the other side of the plateau. The engineer cut the engines and let the train coast. With the noise and vibration of the diesels gone, the only sounds were the squealing of metal on metal and the intermittent hissing of brakes. The wreckage of an old freight south of the tracks served as a warning about runaway trains. As we jolted down the grade, the sensation was like riding in a four-thousand-foot, eight-thousand-ton glider. There were frequent curves, and even on the straight stretches the track wriggled crazily in the locomotive's light.

"If a moose or caribou runs in front of us now, he's dead." The brakeman smiled. "Usually they roll right under the engine and it spits 'em out like hamburger."

Every so often there would be a lurching crash as the back of the train slammed against the front. Out of morbid curiosity, I inquired about derailments. The brakeman said there had been one ten years ago near Cornerbrook. An engine with a boxcar ran head-on into a freight train. The boxcar flew over the locomotive, shearing off the cab and killing the three men inside. "This is just plywood," he explained, tapping on the wall beside me.

We hurtled downhill while a half-moon scythed through clouds and stirred the night into Halloween shapes, its light glancing off a patchwork of marsh water. At the bottom of the plateau, the track skirted a large lake. Through the clouds' shifting angles, slatted moonbeams played over it like a follow spot until the sky sealed up and the only light left belonged to the train.

The ride ended in Cornerbrook, a pulp-and-paper town dominated by a skyline of half a dozen smokestacks. The mill runs night and day, creating a steady roar and an acrid smell that permeates the place if the wind is unfavorable, which it was that night. We arrived at 21:45; it had taken us six hours to cover a distance of 138 miles. Rather than following the freight another 142 miles to Port aux Basques, I caught a bus the next morning. And from Port aux Basques — the terminal where boxcars from the mainland are transferred to narrow-gauge trucks — I took an overnight ferry to the Nova Scotia port of North Sydney, where a passenger train took me on a sleepy and uneventful trip to Halifax.

As Canada's main Atlantic port, Halifax is where a transcontinental rail trip officially begins. It is the point of departure for the Ocean, an overnight express that follows the old Intercolonial and Grand Trunk lines to Montreal, where passengers continuing west can board the daily Canadian to Vancouver. Completed in 1876, the Intercolonial was another steel wedding band that united reticent partners in Canadian Confederation. Running through Nova Scotia and New Brunswick, it connected with the Grand Trunk in the Quebec town of Mont Joli. The Ocean, which began service along the route in 1904, is the country's longest-running passenger train.

Backing on the waterfront, the Halifax station is joined at the hip to an old railway hotel no longer owned by the railway. It is the city's second station. The first was blown to bits along

The Samson, Nova Scotia's first locomotive, in 1838. It traveled a six-mile route between the Albion Mines and the docks at Pictou, Nova Scotia.

with a considerable section of Halifax on December 6, 1917, when a French munitions ship containing five thousand tons of explosive cargo collided with a Norwegian vessel in the harbor Narrows. The blast killed sixteen hundred people, injured eight thousand and left twenty-five thousand homeless. The railway's new dockside terminals, which had just been completed when the blast occurred, were reduced to rubble, and freight cars were sent flying through the air. It was the largest man-made explosion in history until the detonation of the first atomic bomb.

During the Second World War, Halifax was Canada's main terminus for soldiers boarding troopships. They came by trains, as many as twenty-six a day, from all parts of the country. To cope with the traffic, the railway developed one of the continent's first electric switching systems.

Today, most of the rail traffic through Halifax, as elsewhere in the country, is freight. Each day a Nova Scotia quarry sends three hundred-car trainloads of gypsum to the harbor for export. Ships receive potatoes, potash and pulpwood from New Brunswick. And CN runs a vast dockside facility called Autoport, which paints, repairs and modifies imported automobiles for Canadian dealers; it has parking spaces for twenty thousand vehicles. By contrast, the passenger business has suffered from drastic cutbacks in service, especially in the Atlantic provinces, and survives as a concession to the public interest.

Newfoundland's narrow-gauge railway at the Bay of Islands (*c.* 1895).

At the Halifax station, I joined a small queue waiting to board the Ocean. In front of me was a huge man with a fluffy white beard who looked not unlike Santa Claus. He wore a black nylon jacket with large gold lettering across the back that read MAGICIAN. I asked him if he was really a magician, and in a voice that sounded weary from answering the same question too many times, he replied that, indeed, he was.

"I'm an illusionist, really," he added. "I float 'em in the air, saw 'em in half, that sort of thing." As we went to our seats on separate cars of the train, I made a mental note to look him up later on. Meanwhile I headed for the dome car, which is divided into a small bar, a diner and an upstairs observation bubble. The bar is the social center of any Canadian train. It tends to fill up early in the trip, usually with men who drink one beer after another with athletic endurance until they reach their destination. Three young men had set up camp in the Ocean's bar even before we left the station. One was a deer hunter on his way to the woods. The second was a donut baker visiting his parents and the third was a convict returning to his minimum-security prison cell after enjoying a legal unescorted leave.

The deer hunter and the donut man seemed honored to be drinking with a criminal and tried to impress him with their rowdiness. At one point the bartender told them to watch their language. (A train is one of the few public places where you can still hear that kind of old-fashioned reprimand. It is in keeping with the signs in the coach washrooms that prohibit spitting and gambling.) More polite than his companions, the convict possessed the kind of mature composure that only prison or war can instill in a boy of nineteen. He was serving a two-year sentence for an unusual crime. To repay a friend who had stolen some drugs from him, he had broken into the friend's house while he was away and wrecked most of the contents. His favorite part (which elicited shrieks of envy from the deer hunter and the donut man) was firing a twelve-gauge shotgun at the television. Police chased him into a ditch after he sped from the scene in his friend's car, and he later pleaded guilty to charges of assault, mischief and joyriding. "It was the kind of thing you do only once," he explained. He had no regrets. It was raining when he disembarked at Springhill, the Nova Scotia town once famous for its coal-mine disasters. The mines are now closed, and the prison was built to ease local unemployment. As we pulled out, the convict leaned against the station wall, lit a cigarette and waited for a car to take him home to Cell 17.

The train continued north, moving out of the rain, across the provincial border into New Brunswick and past the Tantramar Marshes where pontoon boats thresh wild rice amid flocks of geese, ducks and blue-winged teal. Late in the day, we passed another prison, the maximum-security Dorchester Penitentiary, a walled compound on a hill. Below it is an odd, nine-chimneyed house built by a Yorkshire Englishman in 1913. Aside from the house and the prison, the countryside is quite desolate, not unlike the moors of Yorkshire. On the other side of the tracks flows the serpentine Memramcook River. With the sun down, the river went mauve, and its broad mud banks, left smooth and wet by the far-reaching tides of the Bay of Fundy, gleamed like pewter in the dying light. Occasionally, as it passes through the right place at the right time, a train comes across moments of exceptional beauty . . . inevitably at sunset. After dark, the train turns inside out, and the passengers have nothing to watch but each other.

At dinner I met the magician. He seemed reluctant to talk about his profession at first, but as we sat in the bar and waited for a table in the diner, he suddenly pulled a blue kerchief from his sleeve. He stuffed it through his closed fist a few times then made it vanish. He did it without fuss, as if the kerchief, like a business card, was simply a routine method of establishing credentials. We both ordered veal and sat across from a pulp-and-paper man who ordered halibut.

"Magicians are a dime a dozen," sighed the magician. "You can be a lousy magician and be very successful. It's a business."

I never did find out what the magician had been doing in Halifax. He said it was a business trip, but nothing to do with the magic business. Even after some gentle prodding, he would not elaborate, and it seemed rude to pry further. Just as a slice of landscape flashes by a train window without slowing down for closer scrutiny, a conversation with a passenger—a stranger randomly selected by the train's schedule—sometimes conceals more than it reveals.

That night the train and the magician would continue without me to the St. Lawrence River Valley and southwest to Montreal. I had decided to disembark at the Quebec border. The next morning I would catch another train, one that would trace the rocky coastline of Baie de Chaleur around to the tip of the Gaspé Peninsula.

In the dark, the Ocean rattled across the iron bridge spanning the Restigouche River, which separates Quebec from New Brunswick, and stopped at a small village on the opposite bank. I was the only passenger to get off.

Right: Fishermen in Port aux Basques, Newfoundland. Small fishing boats still play an important role in the local economy of coastal communities in the Atlantic provinces.

The Codroy Mountains in southwest Newfoundland. Violent winds funneling through these mountains have been known to blow freight cars off the narrow-gauge track. Along one especially gusty stretch of track in this area, the railway used to employ a "wind sniffer," who judged if it was safe for trains to pass.

Freight yards at the Ocean Terminals in Halifax, Nova Scotia, the railway's main Atlantic outlet. The original terminals were destroyed on December 6, 1917, when a French munitions ship collided with a Norwegian vessel in the harbor and exploded, killing 1,600 people and obliterating major sections of the port.

Overleaf: Port aux Basques, Newfoundland. In the background is one of the ferries that connects Newfoundland to the mainland port of North Sydney, Nova Scotia.

A CN Rail snowplow in Newfoundland. On the desolate plateau known as the Barrens in the northern area of the island, fifteen-foot snowdrifts are common in midwinter and trains have been stranded by storms for more than two weeks. Caribou herds that roam the plateau have also been known to get in the way of trains.

A long freight train winds across the moors of the Barrens plateau in Newfoundland. Newfoundland's passenger trains have been replaced by buses. The legendary Newfie "Bullet," which would take twenty-four hours to travel 548 miles across the island, made its last trip on July 3, 1969.

Overleaf: A rail worker changes the truck under a car at Port aux Basques, Newfoundland. Freight cars arriving by ferry from the mainland must be transferred from standard- to narrow-gauge trucks. With increasing use of containers, CN Rail is trying to eliminate this time-consuming operation.

This glass etching in a McDonald's restaurant in Moncton, New Brunswick, was designed as a tribute to the city's importance as a rail center and transportation hub for the Atlantic provinces.

The baggage depot in Moncton, New Brunswick.

Overleaf: Canada's longest-running passenger train, the Ocean, passes by Fort Beauséjour near Sackville, New Brunswick, en route from Montreal to Halifax. The fort was completed by the French in 1755 but captured by the British the same year.

VIA

Left: A rail worker in Halifax.

Above: A young rider on one of the last mixed passenger-freight trains to run from St. John's to Carbonear, Newfoundland.

Previous pages: Racing through New Brunswick's verdant Kennebecasis River Valley, en route from Saint John to Moncton.

Above: A freight grazes the shores of the Gulf of St. Lawrence on Newfoundland's windswept west coast.

Pulpwood at the Abitibi-Price paper mill in Grand Falls, Newfoundland. The mill was built in 1909 to provide newsprint for two British publishing magnates, Lords Northcliffe and Rothermere. Today, the forest-products industry is the largest single employer in Canada.

Above: A saddle-tank locomotive in Grand Falls, Newfoundland, was once used for hauling logs.

Left: The Samson, the oldest surviving locomotive in Canada, is displayed behind glass in New Glasgow, Nova Scotia.

Above: A baggage cart and a Budd-car dayliner in the Halifax station.

Right: Wheels dismantled for maintenance in the Halifax yards.

Drying herbs in Dorchester, New Brunswick.

Tarring a roof in Port aux Basques,
Newfoundland.

Left: The Reversing Falls in Saint John, New Brunswick. Twice a day the Bay of Fundy's strong tides force the Saint John River to change direction. At low tide, the river drops over a fourteen-and-a-half-foot ledge; as the tide rises, the water levels equalize and the river becomes calm and flat; at high tide, the onrushing water creates rapids that flow upstream.

Above: A combination plug and sliding door on a CN freight car.

Above: Hayfields alongside the line between Sackville and Moncton.

Left: A tight curve in Newfoundland.

Right: A brakeman eating a home-packed lunch of kippers on the mixed passenger-freight that ran between St. John's and Carbonear until the summer of 1984, when the passenger section was phased out.

Previous pages: The Memramcook River, which winds through the Tantramar Marshes in New Brunswick, becomes a mud flat at low tide. The Bay of Fundy's tides—rising to levels of up to fifty-three feet—are the highest in the world. Nutrients flushed from the marshes by the tides turn the offshore waters into some of the richest fishing grounds in the Atlantic.

Above: The Ocean Terminals at the port of Halifax, Nova Scotia. Resources transferred from train to ship include potatoes, potash, pulpwood and gypsum. Each day three hundred carloads of gypsum (a cement ingredient) from a Nova Scotia quarry arrive at the harbor.

A county fair at Sussex, New Brunswick, seen from a train on the CNR line.

THE ST. LAWRENCE RIVER VALLEY

Above: Quebec City, viewed from a position overlooking the rail yards of Lévis on the south shore of the St. Lawrence River (*c.* 1867).

Left: Super-graphic on a Montreal commuter train in Windsor Station.

The St. Lawrence River points like an arrow into the heart of North America. It ushered in the early explorers and gave momentum to a romance with the west that would be consummated by the CPR three centuries later. Straddling the St. Lawrence today, the province of Quebec, with its French-speaking majority, is the most distinct cultural entity on the continent. Canada's largest province, it extends over an area greater than France, Spain and Germany combined, yet most of its population is still rooted to the broad river valley explored by Jacques Cartier in 1535.

Cartier hoped he had found a convenient passage to the riches of the Orient. Instead, he ended up laying the foundation for the fur-trading colony of New France. And its voyageurs — forging farther west by canoe, to the Great Lakes and beyond — opened up routes that railroad surveyors would retrace two centuries later. Ironically, the railway barons of the nineteenth century were still looking for a shortcut to the Orient: they hoped a transcontinental line would serve as a profitable form of rapid transit for Japanese silk.

Before Cartier managed to locate the mouth of the St. Lawrence, he stumbled into its lower jaw, the curving expanse of the Gaspé Peninsula. Today, a cliff-hugging train route called the Chaleur mirrors his jaunt up the Gaspé coastline. During its thirty-year construction, the line was known as "the railway to nowhere." Instead of making a circuit of the peninsula, it simply stopped at Gaspé, where politicians had promised that a giant grain elevator would transform the town into a major port. But the elevator never materialized, and before the line was completed in 1912 it had generated a series of political scandals that led to the defeat of the Quebec provincial premier, Henri Bourassa. Although the Chaleur never did become a serious freight route for the region (which remains underdeveloped), today it serves as a popular excursion for tourists and a convenient transport link for residents of the isolated coastal communities.

The Chaleur line starts in Matapedia, branching off from the route followed by the Ocean between Halifax and Montreal. A

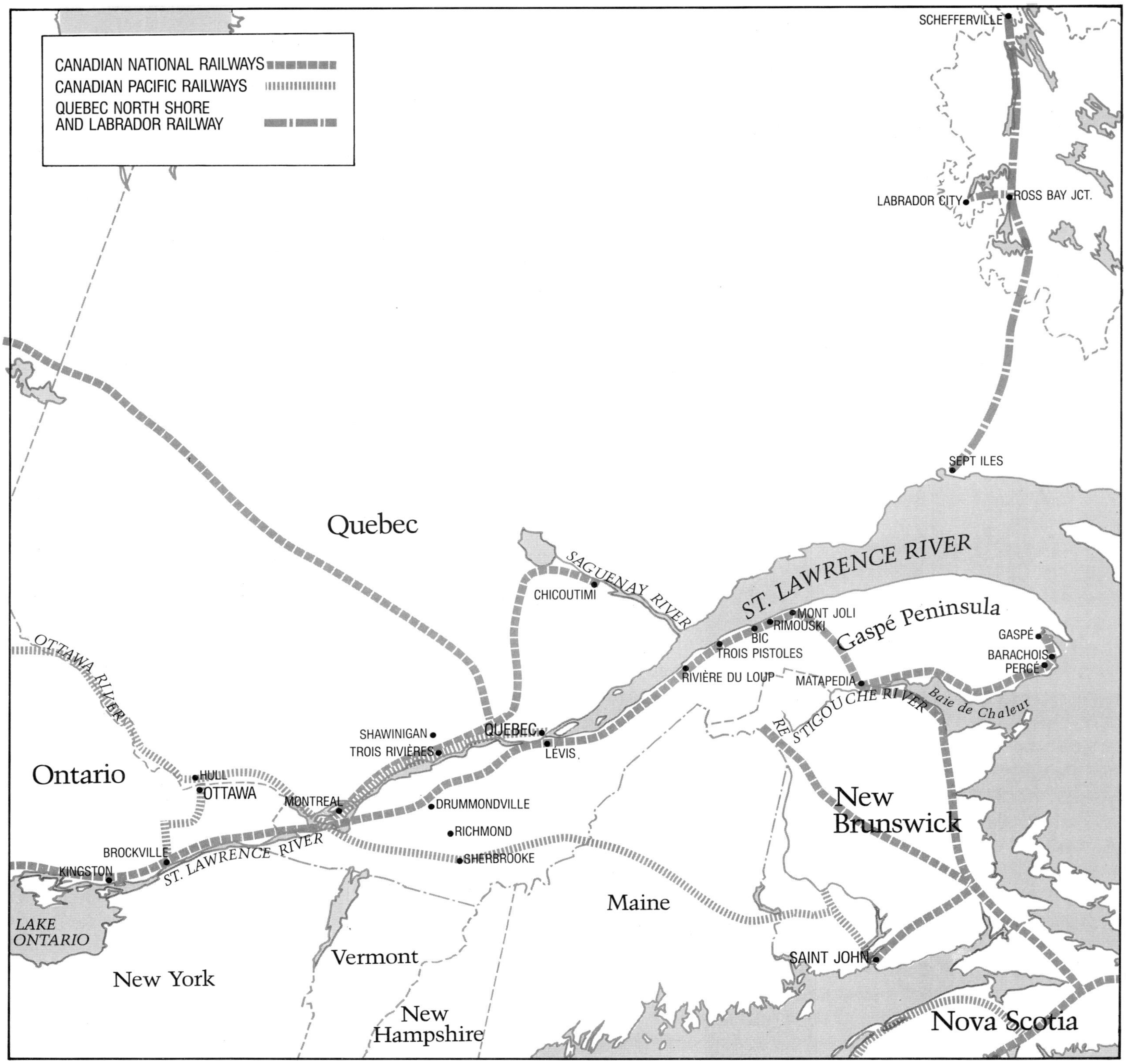

wisp of a village lying in the crook of the Gaspé Peninsula, Matapedia sits on the Quebec side of the iron bridge that spans the Restigouche River. It has a charming frame station, painted gray with red doors and yellow gables. I had to walk only a few paces across the track to find the village's one hotel, whose owner greeted me in French and cheerfully told me his troubles.

The main clientele at the Hotel Restigouche are tourists who come to fish the river, which is considered the finest source of Atlantic salmon on the continent, but the river also poses a problem for both the hotel and the village. During the spring thaw, blocks of ice sometimes pile up under the railway bridge and form a natural dam that causes the river to back up and flood the village. The hotel owner showed me snapshots of his lobby partly submerged, chunks of ice floating by the front door, a canoe gliding across the parking lot. One year the force of the accumulated ice under the bridge was powerful enough to raise the span by seventeen inches. So now, when the ice creeps up, the railway weighs the bridge down with forty freight cars full of granite, which are shunted onto a siding when a train has to pass. When I saw the hotel in daylight, I noticed the rooms were mounted on stilts.

The train that pulled into Matapedia en route to Gaspé in the morning had left Montreal the previous night. The coach was half empty, and passengers were curled up or sprawled under coats and blankets, either asleep or unwilling to admit they were awake. We followed the northern bank of the Restigouche, where the track was walled with a four-foot dike of large rocks to hold back the floods. The river widened into an estuary, turning brown where the silt met salt water, and soon we were riding the edge of the ocean. The train wound slowly along the rim of red and ocher cliffs. To our left, rolling farmland sloped down to the sea in long, perpendicular strips, seigneurial partitions inherited from feudal France. In places the track veered away from the cliffs, leaving narrow margins of carefully cultivated land.

We passed small farmhouses with plastic-covered sheds in the back, clotheslines flapping out to sea, rows of lobster traps neatly stacked, rusted cars laid to rest upside down in cow pastures. We saw beaches the color of sienna, the same rich pigment that runs through the cliffs and the corrugated fields. Fishing boats were sitting on skids by the water and racks of cod were drying in the sun. As we traveled farther along the coast, the farmhouses seemed to get whiter, the ocean bluer.

The passengers were waking up. Across the aisle was a young *Gaspésienne* with the strong features of Basque and Breton ancestors. Her eyes were translucent green as if polished by the sea. She was on her way home to Percé after serving an apprenticeship in *shiatsu* massage at a community college in Rimouski. Percé, the coastal village facing the famous rock with the hole in it, seemed an unlikely place to practice such a sophisticated art. But she said she expected to find clients among the tourists and eventually planned to go beyond massage and into acupuncture, which would mean leaving the Gaspé.

Sitting in front of me were two aspiring beauticians, also going home to Percé. They had been studying hair and cosmetics in Quebec City, and they talked about that picturesque provincial capital as if it were New York.

"Men would follow me around all the time," one of them told me. "In the Gaspé, at least it's safe and the air is clean." Not far from Percé, she pointed to a ship lying several hundred yards offshore. At first glance it appeared to be just anchored there. But the hull was broken in the center, and the bow and stern were jackknifed downward at slight angles. "There was a terrible storm a few months ago," she said, "and the ship ran aground on the rocks. It will probably sit there for years."

The waters of the Gaspé are littered with wrecks, both old and new. Sometimes ships that made it safely past the peninsula met disaster in the deceptive security of the St. Lawrence estuary. One calm, clear night in 1914, fog rolled in from the north shore and enshrouded two ships sailing toward each other near Rimouski. Canadian Pacific's luxury liner, the *Empress of Ireland,* collided with the Norwegian coal ship, *Storstad,* and sank, taking 1,012 passengers and crew to their deaths. There is still a small cemetery near the shore, marked by a silver dome, where 47 unidentified victims of the wreck lie buried.

The beauticians and the masseuse got off at Percé. As the train swung inland to detour around a mountainous cape, the sun creased the evergreen brows of hills to the west. We cut back to the coast, and Bonaventure Island and Percé Rock slid into view. Bonaventure's massive limestone cliffs—a sanctuary for seabirds—were a distant silhouette. Percé's sloping, shiplike form was closer, and its celebrated natural arch (looking not unlike a railway tunnel) was clearly etched against the light.

My excursion on "the railway to nowhere" ended at the town of Gaspé. After a four-hour stopover, I reboarded the same train to go back along the same slow and winding route in the dark—a six-hour, two-hundred-mile trip to the Matapedia junction, where the train would turn north and follow the main line to Montreal.

My roomette was located in the last car, which was called Green Cabin despite the fact that it was blue outside and red inside. The roomette seemed small (6 feet, 5 inches by 3 feet, 7½ inches), but had all the amenities: a chair, a bed that folded into the wall, a porcelain sink, a toilet covered with a padded

A passenger train crossing the frozen St. Lawrence River on the Montreal Ice Railway in 1880.

bench, a large mirror on the sliding door, a cubbyhole marked SHOES, a marvelous panel of old-fashioned toggle switches that controlled four different lights and (best of all) a pouch on the wall by the bed for eyeglasses.

After a sound sleep, I awoke at dawn and raised the blind. A soft light was breaking over the sweeping farmlands of the St. Lawrence Valley. The vast river was perfectly calm, the bluffs of the north shore visible as a mauve silhouette across the water. There were long bacon-strip fields rolling down to small white farmhouses near the riverbank. Punctuating the landscape at sparse intervals were parish churches, slim and elegant with dagger-sharp steeples gleaming silver-gray in the morning light, reminders of a not-so-distant past when the Catholic church was the supreme authority in rural Quebec.

The train raced toward Quebec City along the valley's broad and unobstructed throughway. I scanned the water for whales without seeing any. On Ile aux Basques, an island near Trois Pistoles, furnaces built in the 1500s to extract whale oil have been discovered and restored, but whales are no longer so numerous in the estuary. Church-watching is a more rewarding pastime, especially in Trois Pistoles, which has a church with three spires to match the name of the town.

After the enduring emptiness of the Gaspé and the lower St. Lawrence, Quebec City appeared on the north shore like a vast metropolis, although its population is slightly more than half a million. The train offered the ideal vantage point to watch the skyline unfurl — from the docks and grain elevators of the east end to the spire of Notre Dame Basilica and the fairy-tale turrets of the Château Frontenac towering above the old city's

Laying track on La Tuque branch of the Quebec and Lake St. John Railway in 1907.

Raising the center span of the Quebec Bridge in 1916. The span subsequently collapsed, killing ten workmen.

ramparts. The track runs along the opposite bank, passing under the town of Lévis and skirting tidal mud flats where seabirds poke around for breakfast. My eye followed the citadel walls, along the cliffs General Wolfe's soldiers scaled early one morning in 1759 to surprise the French defendants on the Plains of Abraham and permanently change the course of Canadian history.

Under the cliffs, a long black tanker plied the blue calm like a stick of licorice. Farther upriver, across from the suburb of Ste. Foy, we caught a glimpse of the 3,238-foot Quebec Bridge. Its cantilever span, rising 150 feet above the river, is the longest in the world and was completed in 1917 only after a series of tragic setbacks. During its initial construction in 1907, while a locomotive and a crane loaded with steel rested on its southern cantilever arm, the bridge collapsed, sending seventy-five workers to their deaths. In 1910, work began on a new bridge, which was to be much stronger and nearly twice as heavy as the first. On September 11, 1916, a large crowd assembled to watch the suspended center span being maneuvered into position. But as hoists raised it above the river, a cruciform casting split and released the southwest corner of the span. An eyewitness described what happened: "The center of the span began to buckle and twist like molasses candy. Grinding and roaring, the other end gave way and the mast twisted on its side as though in pain, turned turtle and plunged to the bottom in a great cloud of spray. . . . Bodies were shaken down like apples from a tree, to fall splashing into the river; one man

The Quebec Bridge shortly after the collapse of its center span on September 11, 1916. The bridge, with the longest center span in the world, finally opened on December 3, 1917.

fell from a great height like a ninepin or a wooden doll." Ten men died. A year later a new center span was hoisted into position without incident, and the first train crossed the bridge on October 17, 1917.

West of Quebec City, the main line veers away from the river to bisect Quebec's Eastern Townships, which stretch between the St. Lawrence Valley and the American border. Quaint cottages give way to sprawling dairy farms. Black-and-white cows graze dutifully inert, as if their mouths were wired to the pasture. Viewed from the train, the countryside becomes a series of naive paintings, flat still lifes framed by the moving window. Because people turn to watch a train go by, they are always facing the window, and aside from the waving hands of children, they appear motionless—people, cows, clouds all slide by like ciphers on a continuous roll of music winding through a player piano.

Near Montreal, the pleasant monotony of the plains is broken by a number of small, isolated mountains sprouting from the pancake terrain. They are among eight volcanic cones that were formed 120 million years ago from the bed of the Champlain Sea, which once covered this area. That sea is now reduced to a long, narrow lake straddling the United States-Canadian border, and the volcanoes are worn down to stubs. The most famous is Mount Royal, the forested hub of Montreal.

The train crosses the St. Lawrence Seaway to the island of Montreal via the Victoria Jubilee Bridge, a modified version of a double-tracked, through-truss structure built on limestone piers in 1898. The original Victoria Bridge was a single-track, enclosed tube that was 1.7 miles long and hailed as the eighth wonder of the world when it opened in 1859. Early in the 1880s, during the winter, small trains of a competing line traversed the river on the Montreal Ice Railway, whose tracks were laid across timbers arranged in stone cribs on the ice.

Montreal offers the most dramatic rail entry of any city in Canada. From the bridge, you can see the man-made island where Expo 67's architectural skeletons, notably Buckminster Fuller's geodesic dome, stand as reminders of a faded visionary past. Farther upriver is the green and graceful expanse of the twin-towered cantilever bridge named after Jacques Cartier, the span from which suicidal poets chose to jump when such extreme statements were fashionable.

The skyline itself is an eccentric legacy of the entrepreneurial boom of the fifties and sixties. Among its more bizarre features are Habitat's neo-adobe jumble of waterfront condominiums, Place Ville Marie's white office tower in the shape of a cross and CP's Château Champlain Hotel in the shape of what the most impartial would identify as a cheese grater. One of several nouveau-châteaus built by CP that look nothing like châteaus, the hotel stands in absurd juxtaposition beside the thick stone walls of CP's Windsor Station, which was built in 1889 and *does* look like a château. The station now handles only local trains. The main lines intersect two blocks away under the sprawling concourse of Central Station, which forms the basement of CN's Queen Elizabeth Hotel.

Serving as headquarters for CN Rail, CP Rail and the more recently formed VIA passenger service, Montreal is the historical capital of railway enterprise in Canada. It is also the departure point for the Canadian's three-thousand-mile journey to Vancouver.

Rather than boarding the Canadian in Montreal, I traveled the initial leg to Toronto on one of the frequent express trains that cover the same track. The route is not especially scenic — in fact, it is arguably the most boring stretch of track in the country — but it is classic. A busy shuttle between Canada's two largest urban centers, the route has traditionally served as a sliding index of the rivalry between them. Torontonians travel to Montreal for the Latin magic of the streets and nightclubs. Montrealers come to clean, conservative Toronto to do business or have a quiet time with family or friends. Or so the legend goes.

Leaving Montreal, the train snaked through the decaying underbelly of the city. We glided past row tenements with crumbling back-alley sheds housing fire-hazard furnaces, past windowless brick sweatshops still blackened with the grime of the Industrial Revolution. The view was a stark contrast to the ambitious skyline that greets the passenger arriving from the east. Headed for Toronto — where all obvious traces of urban blight have been fastidiously razed or renewed — we crossed the Ottawa River, then entered Ontario. We kept following the St. Lawrence until, nineteen hundred miles from its mouth, the river widened into the first of the Great Lakes.

Right: Looking for fish at the end of the rainbow — a view from the Chaleur line, the coast of Quebec's Gaspé Peninsula.

The station in Matapedia, Quebec.

Impromptu accommodations in Matapedia.

Overleaf: The Matapedia River Valley. The Matapedia and Restigouche rivers, which flow into the Baie de Chaleur, are the source of North America's finest Atlantic salmon.

Curving steel trestle en route to Gaspé.

The double-tracked through-truss Victoria Bridge in Montreal.

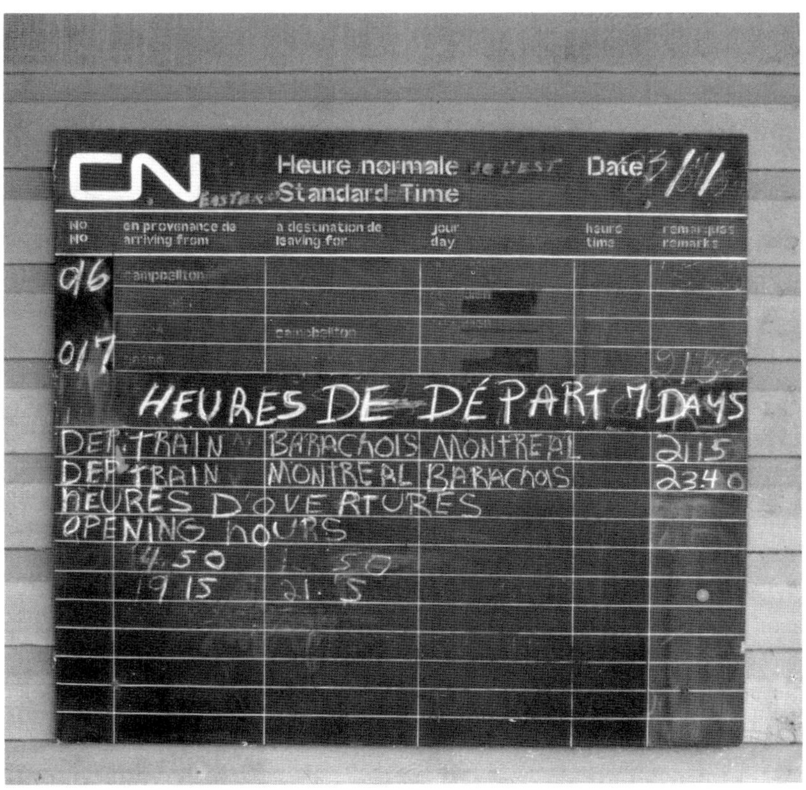

Train schedule at the Barachois station on the Gaspé coast.

Passengers boarding the Chaleur in Matapedia.

Left: The beginnings of the Gaspé Peninsula's Chaleur route, "the railway to nowhere."

Left: Crossing the bridge over Rivière du Loup. The St. Lawrence River is visible in the distance.

Above: The marina and rail terminal are adjacent in the port of Gaspé.

Strip farms near Lévis. The long, narrow partitions of Quebec farmlands—a legacy of seigneurial New France—are unique in North America.

Looking across the Baie de Chaleur toward Quebec's Gaspé Peninsula from the shores of New Brunswick.

Above: The late-afternoon sun casts a shadow as the Chaleur crosses a bridge a few miles from the port of Gaspé.

Right: Boarding a Montreal commuter train in Windsor Station.

900
CTCUM

An executive business car built in 1929 and recently refurbished. Made of heavy steel, it weighs more than one hundred tons and is seventy-seven feet long. It was manufactured in Montreal's Angus shops and is painted in the traditional Canadian Pacific tint, tuscan red.

A twenty-four-hour clock, framed by the royal coat of arms, hangs in Montreal's Windsor Station. Twenty-four-hour time is one thing that distinguishes Canadian railways from their American counterparts. By 1911, all Canadian railways had adopted the system for internal use. And in 1968, public schedules were adapted to it. In the province of Quebec, many theaters, stores and public services use twenty-four-hour time.

Two views of a tunnel in the Gaspé region of Quebec.

A fast-food bus in Rivière du Loup.

The paperwork of tallying tickets occupies much of a conductor's time. Each of the gold bars on his sleeve represents five years of service with the railway.

Overleaf: A CN freight crossing a bridge near Bic, Quebec.

CN
CN

Above: The east end of Montreal's Victoria Bridge at dusk. The traffic signals belong to the roadway that runs parallel to the tracks. With 6,592 feet of iron-work, the Victoria Bridge is the longest railway bridge in Canada. The original bridge, completed in 1859, was a single-track tubular structure. It was replaced with a double-track steel span in 1898, although the original limestone foundations remained. Since then, there have been considerable modifications, notably with the development of the St. Lawrence Seaway in 1959.

Right: When the CPR's Windsor Station was more heavily used, the statue known as the Angel was a popular meeting place. Cast in bronze, the sculpture serves as a memorial to Canadian Pacific employees killed in the First World War, and there are copies in Winnipeg and Vancouver. Windsor Station itself, built in 1889, is a stone fortress whose massive outer walls stand in striking contrast to the airy interior of its main hall—a pillarless open space with a curved expanse of open-girdered ceiling.

4406
4406
CN

THE GREAT LAKES

Above: Toronto's Union Station (*c.* 1875). This building was built in 1873 and replaced an earlier station that dated from the 1850s. The present structure, the third, was opened in 1927.

Left: The grain terminal in Thunder Bay, Ontario. The green vegetation between the tracks is young wheat that has sprouted from spilled grain. Deer are sometimes found grazing here. The trestle above the tracks carries rail cars to a dock where wheat is unloaded directly onto ships.

Ontario is exceptionally well endowed. Not only is it the most prosperous and populous province in Canada, its borders encompass the largest group of freshwater lakes in the world. It is the only province you can enter on a passenger train one day and, after traveling continuously, wake up two mornings later and still be in the same province. It has more track mileage than any other province in the country. During the early boom in Canadian railway construction, three main lines were built across its northern region, a water-riddled expanse of forest, rock and muskeg. Much of the region still remains as sparsely inhabited as when the CPR blasted the first route through the cliffs of Lake Superior a century ago. Ontario's urban population is, in true Canadian fashion, clustered along its southern perimeter. And the rail corridor connecting Quebec with Ontario's southern cities — Sarnia, Windsor, London, Toronto, Kingston and Ottawa — has the busiest passenger traffic in the country.

Standard equipment in the Quebec-Windsor corridor is a new Montreal-built train called the LRC (Light, Rapid and Comfortable). First introduced in 1981, the LRC consists of sleek, modular diesel units and matching coaches with airplane-type seating. Although it is the only new equipment among the country's aging and deteriorating passenger fleet, the LRC has attracted scorn from railway employees because it has been chronically prone to mechanical failure. I have developed my own aversion to the LRC, not on account of any inefficiency, but because it lacks the most basic ingredient of any good train, a bar car. Instead, a waiter wheels a trolley of drinks up and down the aisle, a feature that is advertised as "personal service" but is, in fact, a case of airplane culture inflicting its stay-in-your-seat dogma on rail travel. One of the more interesting things about a train is the opportunity it affords to mingle with strangers in a social setting. Having made the Montreal-Toronto trip countless times, I can attest to the fact that this five-hour jaunt once provided the perfect time frame in which a bar-car liaison could ripen to maturity.

All sorts of gimmicks have been tried on the Montreal-

Toronto run. The most audacious was the Bistro Car, a coach that was gutted and furnished like a gay-nineties saloon complete with a honky-tonk piano player. Introduced in 1968, the Bistro proved immensely popular, perhaps too popular for staid Ontario, and it was eliminated a few years later. From 1969 to 1982, the railway experimented with the Turbo Train, a streamlined express powered by aircraft engines. The Turbo offered a sexy but unstable marriage of technology and social planning. Its best feature was a bar located on an observation deck that was actually an extension of the locomotive cab. Drinks in hand, passengers could look through a glass partition and watch the engineers drive the train. But the Turbo proved too complex to maintain and broke down with such regularity that it was often no faster than the traditional diesel-powered Rapido. It was mothballed in Montreal where, at last report, it is still for sale.

The first train to ply the route between Montreal and Toronto in 1856 was made up of three wooden coaches and a baggage car pulled by a wood-burning locomotive. It made sixty-four stops and it took fifteen hours to cover the 334-mile section of what was then known as the Grand Trunk Railway. As I rode the LRC to Toronto, skimming along welded rail in a straight and uneventful line bordered by Lake Ontario on one side and the Macdonald–Cartier Freeway on the other, it was hard to picture such humble origins. Today, the more memorable items of scenery include the massive General Motors factory in Oshawa — which was the site of the largest carriage works in the British Empire during the last century — and the Pickering generating station, the world's second-largest nuclear-power plant. In the industrial heartland, history leaves no traces.

The LRC rolled into Toronto's Union Station with uncharacteristic punctuality. Though its vintage is relatively recent (1927), Union Station is a convincing monument to the golden age of Canadian rail travel. In the cavernous vault of its lobby, names of station stops are etched in stone along the wall like lists of Roman emperors, and soaring arches suggest a classical grandeur that is marred only if one closely examines the ceiling, which is composed of bricks arranged in a tuneless mosaic. Across the street, the aging gray edifice of CP's Royal York Hotel survives the encroachment of steel and glass. More in the wedding-cake than the château mode, the Royal York was once the pride of Toronto's skyline. Now it is dwarfed by office towers that mirror the sun in shades of black, silver and gold.

When I returned to the station to board the Canadian, the lobby was almost deserted, like a cathedral of some fading denomination. The train pulled out on time, one minute before midnight, and I took a seat in the darkened Plexiglas dome of one of the two observation cars. Leaving the station, we glided slowly past the walls of L'Hôtel. It is Canada's newest railway hotel and — with its Italian marble and cherrywood paneling and crystal chandelier — it harkens back to a lost era of railway opulence.

After L'Hôtel, we passed under the monument that serves as ultimate proof that railways have entered the space age — the concrete spire of the CN Tower. Rising 1,815 feet above the

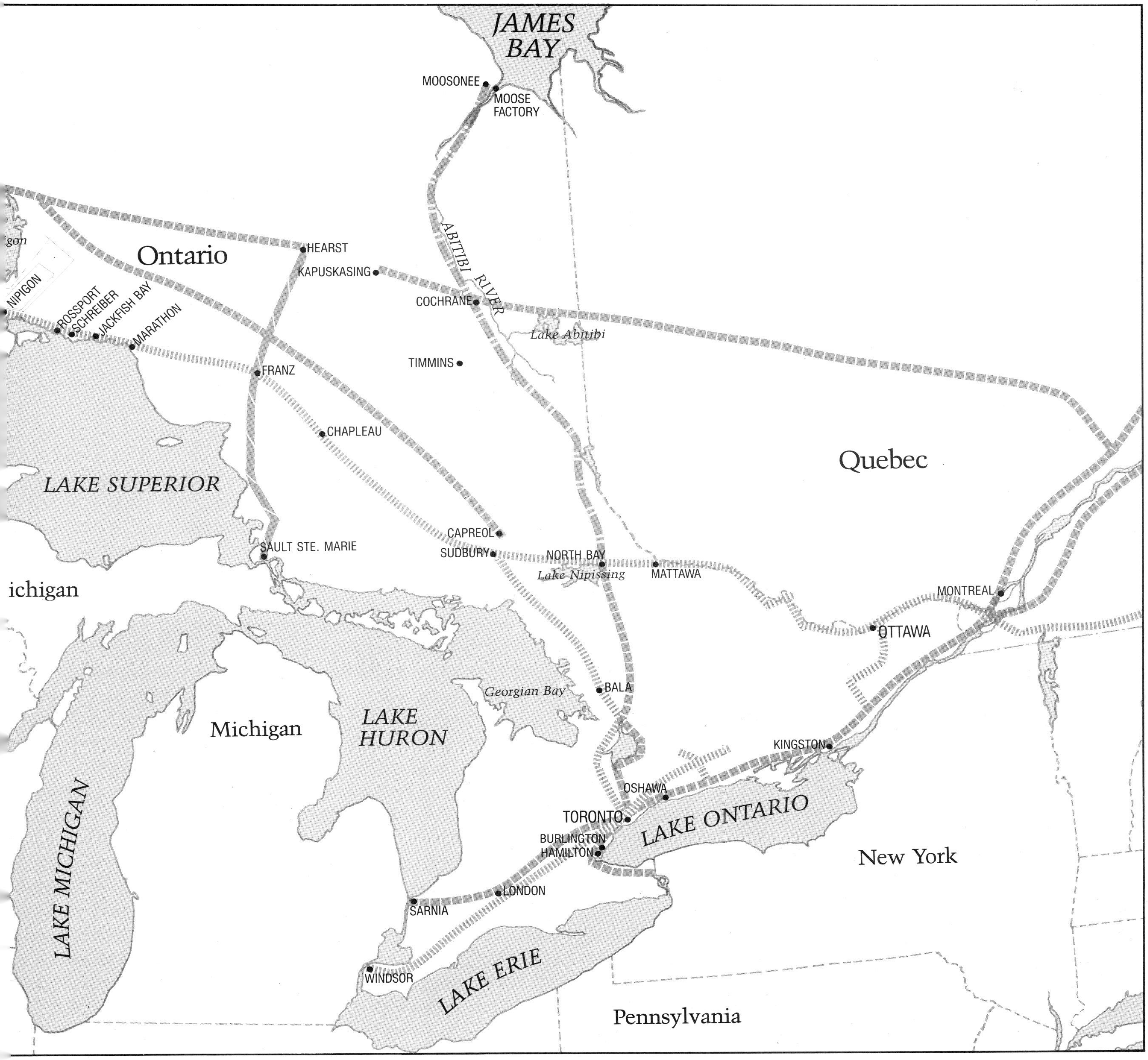

ground, it is the tallest free-standing structure in the world and Toronto's dream come true, an irrefutable icon for the metropolis of three million that takes pride in being Canada's largest city, its financial command center and the hub of its industrial heartland . . . the city that the rest of the country loves to hate.

If Canada was built around a railway masquerading as a nation, Toronto is where the national dream finds the latest fashions for its disguise. The railway was Canada's original medium, and Toronto is very much a media city, a place where high-tech reigns supreme and the streets are as clean and well ordered as a printed circuit. It is also the headquarters of the Canadian Broadcasting Corporation, the network that, along with the railway, receives most of the credit for knitting together the tenuous proposition called Canada. CBC, in fact, was the offspring of a railway. The CNR created the country's first radio network to entertain its train passengers, who listened to the programs on headsets. People began tuning into these "railway stations" on their home radios, and in the 1930s the CBC was formed to take over the network. Trying to bind Canada together with airwaves is perhaps as futile as trying to bind it together with steel. But that is the sort of optimism that thrives in Toronto.

As the Canadian cut north through the city, I squinted to recognize streets in the dark. I have lived in Toronto most of my life, but from the oblique perspective of the rail corridor, everything looked unfamiliar. Before long I was lost. Somewhere in the endless suburbs, I retired to my roomette. It was similar to the one I had in Quebec, except for the sink; it was stainless steel, and one emptied it by folding it into the wall.

I awoke at dawn and rolled up the shade to look out across a rocky moonscape: the outskirts of Sudbury. The place United States astronauts once used to simulate lunar terrain. Catching the sun's first rays was another monument that has found a place in the record books along with the CN Tower: the world's tallest smokestack, which protrudes from the vast Inco smelter, above the world's largest nickel deposit.

Like so many towns along the CPR line, Sudbury was an accident. The line was supposed to run farther south but the locating engineer, acting on his own authority, moved it north.

Although Sudbury was to become an Inco company town, it began as a CPR company town. One day in 1883 a railway employee named Charles Francis Crean noticed a large yellow

A blasting gang cuts through Precambrian rock near Bala, Ontario, in August 1916.

nugget being used as a paperweight in the company store. Crean had it identified as high-grade copper and staked a claim that made him rich.

Sudbury was the last major outpost of civilization that we would encounter until Thunder Bay, more than five hundred miles down the line. In between, we would pass through a scattering of small towns that survive from logging, pulp-and-paper manufacturing, fishing and hunting.

I had expected the landscape to look boring in November, which is a gray month in Toronto, but the northern bush was balanced on the cusp of winter. Although most of the lakes and rivers were not yet frozen, a layer of fresh sunlit snow covered the woods, and the surrounding whiteness made the water look remarkably blue. The smaller ponds were just starting to freeze. Ice, translucent and lined with sutures, covered them like tissue, and in some places new ice encircled patches of rippling water. Lakes flashed by the window in progressive phases of congealment like animation stills. It seemed possible to actually watch the water freeze.

The dome car at the rear of the train was uncrowded. In the summer it is packed, but this was the off-season, when only a select minority chose to travel. There were some Californians, including a family of four on their way back from visiting relatives in the eastern United States, and a real-estate broker who was on the return leg of a transcontinental rail holiday. They had already crossed the country by train from west to east and were all delighted by the experience; they displayed the serene calm that comes from spending a long time on a train. Then there was an Englishman who was in the middle of a trip around the world. He was a strange sort. He kept complaining that there was nothing to look at. He had been traveling by rail since Halifax and had become tired of trees somewhere in New Brunswick.

Natives and surveyors at the Hudson's Bay Company post on the site of what later became Chapleau, Ontario (*c.* 1884).

"Why don't they chop down some of these bloody trees so we can see something?" he asked me. I assured him that without the trees there would be nothing left to see.

Finally there was a young woman from France who frantically jumped from one side of the car to the other to take pictures of lakes. She was determined to get them all, but so many lakes riddle this part of Ontario that she ran through three rolls of film in less than a half hour.

The alternating rhythm of trees and water was dramatically broken by the appearance of what looked like the sea — the enormous expanse of Lake Superior. For much of the next two hundred miles, the track clung to its shoreline, winding through tunnels and along ledges that have been blasted out of granite cliffs a billion years old.

Building the Lake Superior section of the line was a Herculean task. In 1884, the CPR had close to fifteen thousand men and four thousand horses working from Thunder Bay to Lake Nipissing. In the winter, three hundred dog teams were added to the ranks. The men consumed twelve tons of food a day and four tons of tobacco a month. To build a roadbed for the track, they had to blast deep cuts through Precambrian rock and fill muskeg swamps that seemed bottomless. Surveyor Sandford Fleming had proposed an easier route farther north, but here, as in the Rockies, the CPR chose the shortest and most direct path west. By using the shore of Lake Superior, the railway could supply the line by water. Van Horne, in fact, ordered three lake boats built in Scotland, which were sailed across the Atlantic then cut in half to be taken up the St. Lawrence canal system. Prizing self-sufficiency, he also had three dynamite factories

The CPR's Pacific Express en route from Montreal to Vancouver, crossing the Horseshoe Trestle near Schreiber on the north shore of Lake Superior in 1886. During the 1890s many wooden trestles, including this one, were replaced with earth fills.

A rock cut near Jackfish Bay on Lake Superior's north shore in 1885. Almost every inch of the route in this area had to be blasted. Freshly laid track was often washed away or destroyed by rock slides.

built on Superior's north shore, each capable of producing a ton of explosives a day. The railway was at war with the land and it needed a lot of ammunition.

In summer the workers were tortured by the insects and the heat, but the winters were worse. Temperatures dropped to forty and fifty degrees below zero, and snow piled up to five feet deep. Sometimes it drifted so high that the workers, unable to find the grade, laid tracks directly onto the snow, only to have the spring thaw expose places where they had missed the grade entirely.

The men slept in narrow bunkhouses thrown together with spruce logs, and there were camps of Italian immigrants working on subcontracts who lived in hovels without floors or windows. The universal anesthetic among the navvies was whiskey, which was illegal and distributed by bootlegging gangs who enforced a frontier justice with revolvers, rifles and bowie knives. Whiskey and dynamite blazed the CPR's trail through the bush, and no one paid much attention to the scenery. As Pierre Berton points out in *The Last Spike*, "To the men on the job . . . the scenery was only a nuisance to be moved when it got in the way."

Nevertheless, the route that Van Horne called "two hundred miles of engineering impossibilities" offers a spectacular ride. It begins around Marathon, a pulp-and-paper town where logs are heaped like toothpicks beside the track. There are still relics of wooden flumes there, and of the long aqueducts once used to float logs down from lumber camps in the hills. Marathon is looking forward to a new era of prosperity. A lucky prospector recently staked a claim in the vicinity for what will become the largest gold mine in Canada.

It was tempting to imagine what other treasures could lie buried beneath the stern profile of the Precambrian Shield, as we passed under the cliffs that rim Superior. Tinged red and ocher, these faceted bluffs with overhangs jutting high above the track looked almost alive, and in a sense they are. Sections of track are protected by slide-detector fences strung with wires that trip a warning signal when struck by falling rock. The cliffs are most fragile in the spring, when ice that has expanded through cracks in the rock suddenly melts.

The Canadian proceeded gingerly along the shoreline. It was getting dark as we rounded the horseshoe curve of Jackfish Bay. It was one of the last sections of track to be completed, and construction costs soared as high as $700,000 a mile — at a time when wages were only $1.50 an hour. Including Jackfish, there were four gaps in the line through Ontario in early 1885. The CPR was on the verge of bankruptcy with no solution in sight when the North West Rebellion, led by Louis Riel's Métis and Indian forces, broke out in what is now Saskatchewan. The government used the CPR's new railway to rush three thousand troops west in two weeks. They quickly quelled the rebellion, and the government bailed out the CPR, which had suddenly acquired national prestige. The troops, however, did not have a pleasant trip. They rode through sub-zero weather in open flatcars and had to trek across long stretches of glare ice to skirt unfinished segments of track along Lake Superior.

Comfort on the CPR has improved substantially since 1885,

although it has declined from the luxurious standards set some thirty years ago. Then the railway's cuisine and service were legendary, from the silver-plate table settings to the pan-fried trout freshly caught in Lake Superior and loaded onto the train at a fishing village. Today the train serves catered meals, but at least they are cooked to order rather than warmed in a microwave oven.

As we headed toward Thunder Bay I retired to the bar. There are actually two bars on the Canadian, one in each of the dome cars. The middle dome car, which serves as a divider between the coaches and the sleeping cars, is open to everyone, including coach passengers. The rear dome car, at the very back of the train, is reserved for sleeping-car passengers. It is a special parlor car with a rounded stern that always forms the tail end of the Canadian. Each model is named after a national or provincial park, in our case Algonquin Park. Downstairs from its dome is a lounge with armchairs arranged around giant ashtrays. Farther forward is a bar walled with a partition of cut-glass floral designs inlaid with tiny lights. Some of the parlor cars still have murals painted by Canada's celebrated Group of Seven. But many, including the Algonquin, have had their murals removed and enshrined in more formal surroundings. The parlor car is a good place to have a civilized conversation, but the middle dome car, with its more proletarian clientele, is often livelier.

We arrived in Thunder Bay about midnight. The Englishman was highly impressed by what he could see of the lakehead port, especially the rows of huge grain elevators. There are twenty-five of them with a total capacity of a hundred million bushels, enough to fill a hundred ships.

The eastern terminal for prairie grain and the largest pulp-and-paper center in Canada, Thunder Bay is where the St. Lawrence Seaway ends. The Prairies, however, do not begin for another 350 miles. All night we traveled through the Ontario wilderness, shadowing the crooked canoe routes that had led the fur traders west, and crossing muskeg so deep that the track had to be laid over a "mattress" of floating timbers. When a freight train passes over it, the mattress sags noticeably under the weight, and from a distance the front of the train appears to be planing slightly, like the prow of a boat.

Sometime during breakfast, two days and 1,433 miles after entering the province, the Canadian finally passed out of Ontario. The Englishman was relieved.

The interior of a parlor car on the Grand Trunk Railway at the turn of the century.

Right: As the train approaches Toronto, the porter readies the luggage for disembarking.

The 1,250-foot smokestack of the Inco nickel smelter casts a pall over the moonscape surrounding Sudbury. Slag from the Inco mines is used throughout the region as ballast for the railway tracks.

Rossport, a village on the north shore of Lake Superior, was an important stop in the early days of train travel. Here, fresh lake trout were loaded onto dining cars and pan-fried for the next meal. Today, the meals on the Canadian, though fresh-cooked, are catered, and the train no longer stops in Rossport.

Overleaf: The Polar Bear Express crosses a wooden trestle just after pulling out of Moosonee for its return trip south. The Polar Bear route of the Ontario Northland Railway—extending 186 miles from Cochrane to Moosonee—follows the old canoe routes of the Abitibi and Moose rivers to their outlet at James Bay. Still the only land-transport link to Moosonee, the line was completed in 1932.

1517
Rail
Services
1517
Ontario
Northland

Ontario
Northland

The royal train, on which Queen Elizabeth and Prince Philip rode during their visit in September 1984. The royal standard flying from the locomotive cab is a courtesy flag, not an operating flag. (Operating flags include the white flag, which denotes an extra train that is not listed, and the green flag, which means that the second section, drawn by another locomotive, is following.)

Dining car on the Canadian. Built in 1955 by the Budd Company of Philadelphia for the CPR, the car features glass partitions etched with drawings of Canadian birds. Although transcontinental dining has lost its legendary luxury, a standard of service is still maintained on the Canadian.

Left: The Canadian heading east from Thunder Bay in the late fall. The aspens and poplars that dominate the landscape are typical of second-growth forests, which have replaced conifers destroyed by logging and fire throughout northern Ontario.

Above: Railway track, road and dock give way to the quiet beauty of a northern Ontario landscape.

The observation dome of the Canadian, which offers the longest dome-train ride in the world. Each train is equipped with two stainless-steel dome cars—one in the middle for coach passengers, one at the end for sleeping-car passengers. The cars belong to a fleet of 173 passenger cars that the CPR purchased from Budd Company of Philadelphia in 1955.

A typical trackside view in northern Ontario. Such landscapes were made famous by the paintings of Canada's Group of Seven, some of whom created murals to decorate interiors of the domed Park cars of the Canadian.

Overleaf: A train from Moosonee unloads at Cochrane. The Ontario Northland Railway's mixed passenger-freights pick up and drop off fishermen, hunters and trappers at unscheduled points all the way along the line. Boxcars are allotted for canoes and camping gear.

2011
40-6
9-2
10-0
3712
C

Ontario Northland
ONT. 2547
1802

Above: The Canadian stops at a camp in the northern Ontario bush to drop off supplies and passengers.

Left: Passenger at Cochrane. It is said that a dog in White River lived off scraps from dining cars, and could distinguish the whistle of a passenger train from that of a freight.

Above: A Cree Indian freight canoe is the only regular transport from Moosonee to the island of Moose Factory across the river.

Right: This mobile snack bar in Moosonee has a bilingual menu—the language on the left is Cree.

Above: The Canadian makes an unscheduled stop to drop off moose hunters.

Cree-language characters on the side of an Ontario Northland Railway car that now serves as a museum in Moosonee.

Super-graphics on the Ontario Northland Railway.

Work gang.

Cemetery at Moose Factory, the first British settlement in Ontario. Moose Factory was founded in 1673 as a Hudson's Bay Company fur-trading post. The French voyageur Chevalier Pierre de Troyes, arriving by canoe, captured the post in 1686, and Britain regained possession in 1730.

Overleaf: The Canadian winds through the lake-riddled terrain of northern Ontario. About seventeen percent of the province is covered by water.

Slide-detector fences along the north shore of Lake Superior near Marathon. Rocks falling through the fence will trigger a signal for the train to stop. Carving the original CPR roadbed out of Superior's granite ramparts was an engineering feat almost as formidable as blasting the route through the Rockies.

Near Campbellville, Ontario.

ROYAL YORK

The conductor of the 1984 royal train.

One of its dining-car stewards.

Opposite: Toronto's skyline, featuring the sixteen-hundred-room Royal York Hotel, which Canadian Pacific opened in 1929. Below it are Union Station and the city's original freight yards, now slated for redevelopment. The railway car in the immediate foreground is the Cape Race, an observation-solarium car that was built for CPR's transcontinental service in 1929. It now belongs to the Upper Canada Railway Society.

Above: Brakeman's view from a caboose.

Right: Brake wheel on a freight car.

RELEASE
APPLY

Muskeg near Chapleau in northern Ontario. This kind of swampy terrain posed serious problems for those who laid track through the wilderness of the Precambrian Shield. In places, railway builders drove 150-foot piles into muskeg without hitting bottom. Even today, portions of track crossing muskeg are "mattressed" over layers of logs.

Grain elevators at the Thunder Bay terminal. Canadian railways move about forty million tons of grain a year, and nearly half of it goes through Thunder Bay. Before being loaded on ships, most of it passes through one of the port's twenty-five concrete elevators, where it is weighed, graded, cleaned, treated if necessary and stored until shipment.

PIONEER
FROSTY
TREAT
SUNDAES
PECAN & WALNUT 20¢ EXTRA
SUNDAES 1.30-1.50 PINTS 1.75 QUARTS 3.20
MILK SHAKES 1.30-1.50 FLOATS 1.30 1.50 1.70
BLIZZARDS 1.90 1.70 DRINKS .55 .85 1.10
BANANA SPLITS 2.00
CONES .60 .85 1.10 DIP 10¢ EXTRA
MILK SHAKES
ENJOY
Coca-Cola
FANTA
OPEN
Sprite
Coca-Cola
VANILLA SOFT ICE CREAM
HAVE A NICE DAY

THE PRAIRIES

Above: Laying track for the CPR's drive across the Prairies in the early 1880s.

Left: A grain elevator in southern Saskatchewan. More than four thousand of these wooden warehouses are scattered along rail lines throughout the Prairies. Local farm trucks unload their grain at the elevator, where a conveyor belt carries it to the top of the appropriate bin. The grain is dumped by gravity into rail cars. Elevator workers wear protective masks. In this case, ice cream is available as an antidote to the dust.

Nowhere in Canada has the railway had a more profound impact than on the Prairies. Before the arrival of the CPR, the vast southwest plains now contained by Manitoba, Saskatchewan and Alberta were an unfenced sea of grass. It was in this virgin territory that the CPR played God: it fostered some eight hundred villages, towns and cities and determined, often arbitrarily, the shape of a new society.

If the railway had followed the more northern route originally proposed by the surveyor Sandford Fleming, civilization on the Prairies would have evolved quite differently. Fleming's route followed the footsteps of the fur traders, cutting northwest of Winnipeg, reaching Edmonton by way of the fertile, wooded valley of the North Saskatchewan River and crossing the Rockies through the Yellowhead Pass. But the CPR, overriding critics who argued that much of the land in the southwest was too dry to be arable, tossed out a decade of survey work and opted for a southern route, partly because it was shorter, and also because it would discourage American competitors from poking branch lines across the border. Later, both the Grand Trunk Pacific and the Canadian Northern Railways built lines along Fleming's northern route, which eventually became part of the CNR. But it was the CPR that provoked the first wave of settlement on the Prairies and left the most indelible impression.

As its officials set out from Winnipeg in 1881 to chart the exact path the track would follow, there was a frenzy of land speculation. An advancing army of squatters tried to second-guess where the main stations (and thus the new towns) would be located. Sometimes the railway men simply sidestepped the speculators and put their stations in the least likely places.

The company's iron grip on this new territory was not confined to the tracks. The federal government had endowed the CPR with twenty-five million dollars and twenty-five million acres of land. Because the mountain and the Great Lakes regions were provincially owned (and also largely unfit for farming), the contract said all the land had to come from the Prairies.

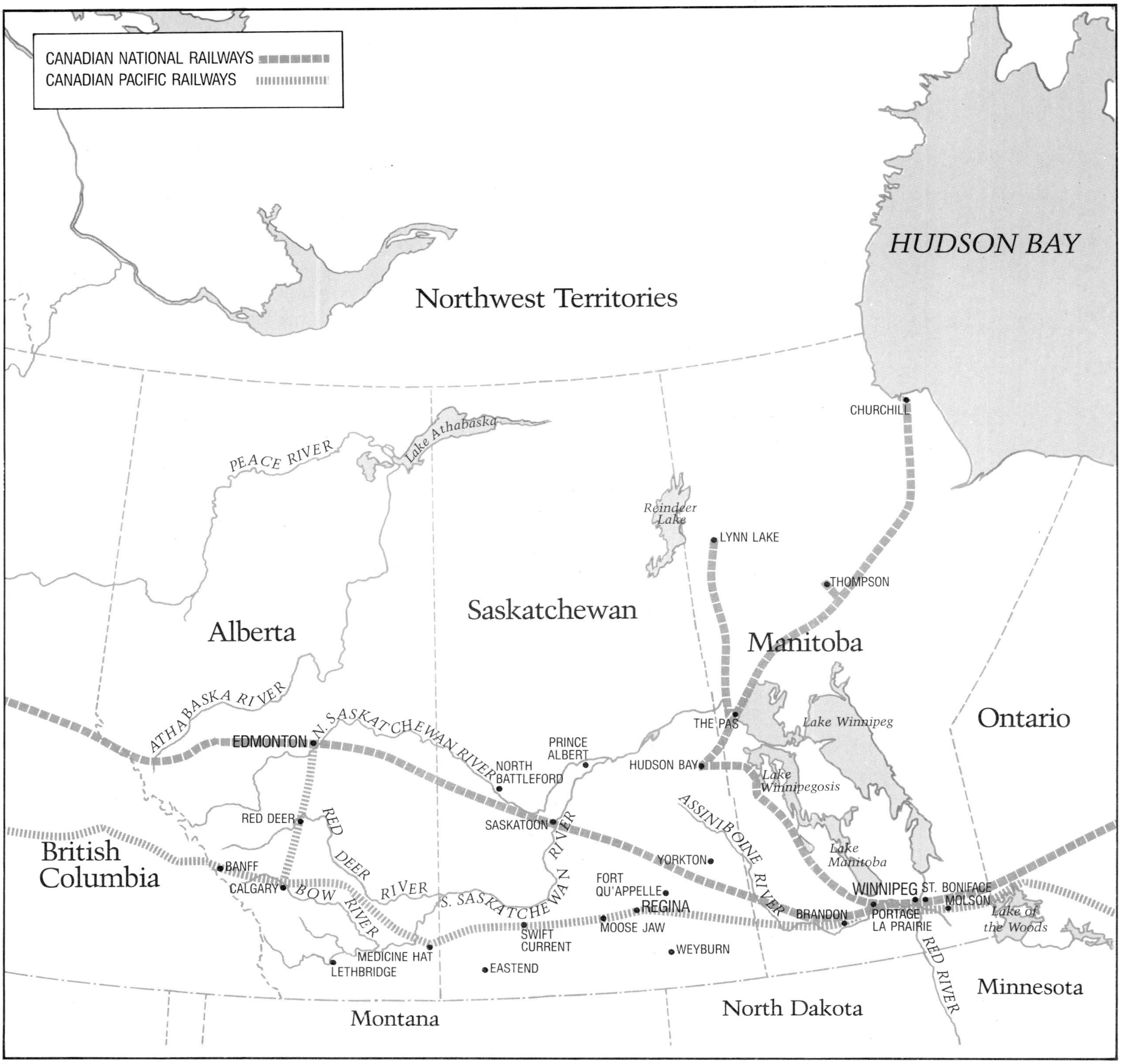

Although the company was expected to stay within a forty-eight-mile belt along the rail line, it was free to choose Crown land from anywhere between the Red River and the Rockies.

Settlement was slow at first, especially on the dry plains of southern Saskatchewan and Alberta. But after the turn of the century, new strains of wheat and better farming techniques turned the Prairies into the breadbasket of the world. The railway sprouted a myriad of spur lines, capillaries siphoning grain from enterprising little farm towns that popped up almost overnight.

The boom ended with drought, dust and depression in the

Roundhouse in Medicine Hat, Alberta, in the 1890s.

Dirty Thirties. Some of the more far-flung communities vanished as quickly as they had appeared. Others hung on for another generation or two only to find themselves bypassed by a new age of superhighways and mechanized farming. In recent years, the railways have continued to recede, amputating minor tributaries that led only to ghost towns. The durable towns and cities still cluster along the main CP and CN arteries, conduits that pulse with a constant lifeblood of grain, coal, potash . . . and, twice a day, slipping through the busy freight schedules, a passenger train flashes by.

As the Canadian moves from Ontario into Manitoba, the transition from the Shield to the Prairies is radical. You can miss it if you have your head turned. One moment you are looking at the Shield's rhythmic variations of rock and evergreen; suddenly they turn into marshy grassland studded with deciduous trees; a few minutes later the prairie begins as an expanse of black-loam farmland. Until eight thousand years ago, most of southern Manitoba was covered by the world's largest freshwater lake — larger than all the Great Lakes combined—and its silt deposits have made the Red River area especially fertile.

At the junction of the Red and Assiniboine rivers, about two hours inside the Manitoba border, Winnipeg appears quite abruptly, a city rising from an empty plain. We crossed the Red River alongside a slow-moving freight train (because of the tremendous volume of eastbound grain, the line between Winnipeg and Thunder Bay is double-tracked), and the bridge led us directly into the downtown, where a huge brick peanut factory emblazoned with a sign reading NUTTY CLUB served as a bizarre welcome mat.

Winnipeg is a curious hybrid. It looks as if two cities have been randomly shuffled together, one made of gleaming office towers and malls, the other of crusty old bank buildings and stores with fading signs hand-painted on brick.

First settled by Scottish immigrants in 1810, Winnipeg boomed when the CPR made it the railhead for its drive west. Gold-rush fever swept through the town, although the only gold to be had was real estate. Its value multiplied beyond all reason as hundreds of speculators sold land back and forth. By 1882 property was more expensive in Winnipeg than in Chicago, selling for up to two thousand dollars a foot. Buildings mushroomed; hotels were jammed; bars flowed with champagne. And real-estate agents appeared all over the country with pieces of Manitoba for sale.

The boom lasted less than a year. The bubble burst in the spring of 1882 when Winnipeg was hit with the worst flood in memory. The Red River washed out bridges, submerged the rail line and turned the most prized lots into quagmires. And while the town was cut off from the outside world for three weeks, land buyers were already eyeing an exotic new frontier at Fort Edmonton. About seventy-five percent of Manitoba's businesses collapsed after the floodwaters receded. Winnipeg recovered and became Canada's seventh largest city, but never again was it so rambunctious.

Today Winnipeg is a major rail center, the nexus through which all the main lines are threaded. From its station, passengers can take the Polar Bear Express to the Hudson Bay outpost of Churchill, the Panorama to the Pacific port of Prince Rupert or the Canadian to Vancouver or Montreal. All passenger traffic passes through the CN station downtown, which makes a simple attempt at grandeur with heavy pillars, a domed azure ceiling and a rotunda.

More intriguing though, is the old CP station, built in 1904, which is now used only for administrative offices. Located at the other end of town amid a wasteland of rooming houses, pawnshops and beverage rooms, it is a stately brick edifice with an imperial facade of massive limestone blocks. You walk through the portals and step into a grand hall with fat, Miami-pink pillars propping up a ceiling bordered with gilt rococo motifs. The ceiling itself is cheap acoustic tile, but the floor is hand-laid glass mosaic.

The ghost station seems eerily intact, from the polished brass railings to the unlit neon signs announcing LADIES, TICKETS, BAGGAGE. . . . It is as if one could simply throw a switch and the place would come back to life. Next door, however, there is a park on the site where CP's Royal Alexandra Hotel once stood. The hotel had been built solidly: the demolition company that knocked it down in 1971 almost went broke from the effort. Grandeur passes quickly on the Prairies, and empires are no longer measured in stone and brick. But across from the CN station, the old Fort Garry Hotel still stands, another in the château style, built by the Grand Trunk Pacific Railway.

Spanning the Oldman River in Alberta, the CPR's Lethbridge Viaduct is the highest railway bridge in Canada. Here, the last of thirty-four steel spans is hoisted into place in 1909.

The CPR station in Winnipeg, Manitoba, was completed in 1904. It is now used only for administrative offices.

A calm settled over the train as we ventured west from Winnipeg. In the Prairies there are no obstacles and few landmarks, except the brightly painted grain elevators, which break the flatness with the same frequency as church spires in Quebec. Passengers casually scanned the landscape every so often in case it had changed. The slightest deviations from the horizontal invited inspection. The eye lingered on a barn, a hill, a clump of trees or perhaps a truck driving along the highway a little slower or faster than the train.

The Englishman who hated trees loved the Prairies. "At least you can see something," he said, "a farm, a house — *something*. Anything is better than all those trees." The Englishman, it turned out, was predisposed to farms because he had grown up on one. In fact, after his father died he had sold the family farm, moved to the tax-sheltered Guernsey Islands off the coast of France and was now traveling around the world on the profits and feeling quite guilty about it. He told me he was headed to Australia, New Zealand, Hong Kong "and then out to Abba Abba or someplace where they've got people as black as coal with white robes wrapped around their heads." He did not seem to be looking forward to it. But he felt at home with the Prairies, even though it was late in the season and they were not looking their best.

The harvested fields were barren save for a scattering of leftover haystacks. Not long after Winnipeg, fog rolled in, cutting the legendary unlimited view down to a few hundred yards. The Prairies, of course, should be viewed in August, when the wheat becomes a sea of rippling textures changing shades with the wind, variations of burnished gold under a blue-enamel sky, and distant grain elevators shimmer in the heat, the sole landmarks against a horizon circumscribing 360 degrees of infinity.

The Englishman was curious about the grain elevators, which he called sheds. He did not believe me at first when I explained that farmers trucked grain to the elevator, where it was carried up by conveyor belts and later dumped into rail cars. He had been impressed by the large concrete elevators in Thunder Bay, but the wooden ones, these cherished icons of Canadiana, he found silly.

About three hours west of Winnipeg, we stopped at Brandon beside a main-street phalanx of old brick buildings housing seed companies and farm-machinery firms. Like the grain elevators, they seemed monumentally tall in such flat surroundings, as if they were specifically designed to make a mark on the horizon. Known as Wheat City, Brandon owes its existence to a CPR maneuver to outflank land speculators. It was born in 1881 when the railway chose its site for a station, although a more predictable place would have been two miles east at Grand Valley, where the track was to cross the Assiniboine River. Tents, shacks and even a canvas hotel had sprung up in Grand Valley as land grabbers prepared for the boom they considered inevitable. But then a homesteader who occupied the spot where the station was to be built was goaded by speculators into demanding an inflated price for his land. The CPR's chief engineer, General Thomas Rosser, a Virginian who had made his name leading Confederate cavalry charges in the American Civil War, was not about to be pushed around. He simply moved

Calgary in 1884. Just one year earlier, when the CPR first reached Calgary after laying track across the Prairies, the townsite consisted of a log fort and a collection of squatters' shacks.

the station, effectively killing off the ambitious little community of Grand Valley and giving birth to Brandon. Rosser, however, was later fired for doing some speculating of his own.

Brandon was the first of the CPR towns. As we continued west, crossing from Manitoba into Saskatchewan, we would pass through many others—communities that were so much empty space on the prairie a little more than a century ago. As with Brandon, their locations were often illogical. Fort Qu'Appelle, located in a wooded river valley, was considered the obvious site for the new capital of the northwest, but the railway veered south of it. The site chosen for the town that would become Regina, now the capital of Saskatchewan, was an arid and treeless plain beside the Pile o' Bones Creek. The creek's name, translated from the Indian name Wascana, is derived from the thousands of bleached buffalo bones that were once piled along its banks, where the Indians used to drive the buffalo into a corral to be slaughtered.

The Indians were the only real obstacle the CPR encountered in its push across the Prairies, and they were easily displaced. Before the railway's arrival, the white man had already irreparably poisoned the Indian's way of life with firearms and firewater traded for buffalo hides. By 1880 the great buffalo herds were decimated and the natives were starving. Bisecting the ancient hunting grounds of the Blackfoot and Cree, the iron road terminated whatever freedom the Plains Indians had left. A race of proud hunters was forced onto reservations and told to become farmers.

The only significant resistance to the railway came from the Blackfoot reserve near Calgary. Chief Crowfoot, leader of the Blackfoot nation, sent envoys to tell the foremen that seven hundred braves would attack if construction proceeded any farther. The CPR ordered a halt to the work, and Albert Lacombe, a missionary who had established a legendary reputation with the Blackfoot band, was sent to placate them. Lacombe convinced Crowfoot to let the railway through in exchange for extra lands.

Steel advanced across the Prairies at an astounding rate, averaging about twenty miles per week. The line was built telescopically, with the track serving as its own supply line. Each morning two trains would set out for the End of Track, each loaded with ties, rails, fishplates and spikes. The tracklayers, working fifteen-hour shifts, became precision teams, and before they reached the Rockies, one group set a record: they laid 6.38 miles of finished track in a single day.

For a passenger on the Canadian, crossing the Prairies is an exercise in monotony or tranquility, depending on one's point of view. For me, they seemed to flash by in a twinkling. I slept through half of Saskatchewan and a good part of Alberta. My last memory before waking up on the outskirts of Calgary was stopping in Moose Jaw shortly before midnight. Moose Jaw has probably the best-preserved western station in the country. It is a brick building with arched windows and an ornate interior of carved friezes. A brass clock hangs above an old-fashioned ticket wicket, which faces a waiting room lined with wooden pews. Along one wall, a snack bar has been converted into a shrine of railway memorabilia, complete with a model train set that follows a circuit around the counter top. Outside the front door is a western main street that looks as if it has not changed in decades.

The Canadian changed crews at Moose Jaw and the new conductor talked my ear off about how things used to be — when the station was not a museum piece but a bustling center for farmers, when it had a dining room that was considered the finest in town. But Moose Jaw's fortunes, like those of so many other Prairie towns, were fading.

"Now you're an easterner," said the conductor, looking up at me from a table littered with triplicate tickets and forms. "Well, this is where all your jelly beans come from." Jelly beans? "Your natural resources. We sell you our wheat, our minerals, our oil and gas, and you sell us your manufactured goods. But the farmer can't afford to buy your equipment today. He can't even afford to keep up the mortgage payments on his farm."

The conductor had the pear-shaped physique and country-doctor countenance that are standard gauge among men who have worked on trains for more than thirty years. While jotting down ticket numbers, he delivered a full-scale speech about eastern politicians and industrialists who were driving the Prairies into the dust, about railway executives who were killing off the passenger trains for the sake of smoother freight runs, about the general decline of civilization. . . .

In the night we crossed into Alberta, passing through the dry short-grass country, where wheat farming gives way to cattle ranching, and descended the incline to Medicine Hat, which

British visitor Rudyard Kipling described as a place "with all Hell for a basement." Although he was referring to the huge natural-gas deposits under the city, Medicine Hat's history is not without a few supernatural undercurrents. There are various legends about the origin of its name. According to one, a gust of wind caught the magical hat of a Cree medicine man during a battle with a Blackfoot band and sent it flying into the Saskatchewan River. The Cree saw it as a dire omen and fled.

The Canadian cut northwest across Alberta and pulled into Calgary in time for breakfast. An oasis of steel and glass poised on the edge of the prairie, Calgary was founded by the railway but transformed by the oil companies. In the 1960s and early 1970s, the Alberta oil boom turned it into a city of the future, with office towers competing for supremacy in a growing skyline. But when the bottom dropped out of world oil prices, Calgary, like so many prairie boom towns of a previous generation, found itself all dressed up with nowhere to go. Some of the office towers now stand half empty.

There is a sanitized newness to the downtown. The railway station is buried in its core, camouflaged under the bric-a-brac geometry of a shopping mall. Directly above it soars the Calgary Tower, a concrete needle crowned with a revolving restaurant. Rising 626 feet from the pavement, it was the highest structure in the city when it was erected. Now, surpassed by taller office towers, it looks disturbingly squat.

I joined the Americans and the Englishman at the summit of the Calgary Tower for breakfast. The Englishman was staggered by the sheer quantity of food that arrived on his plate: bacon, sausages, pancakes, eggs, toast and muffins. The Americans marveled at the low price. We all admired the view. To the west, floating like a mirage above the horizon, were the snow-capped peaks of the Rockies, looking almost diaphanous against a clear morning sky.

Right: Brandon, Manitoba.

CP 434693

Wheatfields in southern Alberta. In the background is a 1,891-foot railway viaduct spanning the Oldman River twenty miles west of Lethbridge.

A painting of Banff National Park by the Group of Seven's A.J. Casson adorns the wall of a lounge car on the Canadian. In the early 1950s, the CPR commissioned artists from the Royal Canadian Academy to paint murals for eighteen domed cars that it had ordered for the Canadian. Named after national and provincial parks, they are known as Park cars. The CPR used to advertise the Canadian as "an art gallery on wheels."

Overleaf: A CP Rail freight yard in Winnipeg, Manitoba. Because all Canada's transcontinental main lines are threaded through Winnipeg, it is one of the country's most important rail centers. The city, which began as a Scottish settlement in 1812, boomed with the arrival of the CPR in 1881 and became headquarters for the railway's drive west and the colonization of the Prairies. Today, western resources, such as grain, potash, sulphur, oil and natural gas, pass through Winnipeg en route to eastern markets.

CASH & CARRY DEPOT
CP Rail
PROCOR
UNPX
120390
P Rail

VERMONT
RAILWAY
Canadian Pacific

Tank cars at the Medicine Hat yards are used to carry natural gas.

The CPR in southern Manitoba.

Left: Hand-tooled leather decorates the bar in the Canadian's Sibley Park car.

Above: A trainman beside the Canadian.

Canada
Canada

PIONEER
POOL

Previous pages: Grain elevators form the skyline of Eastend, Saskatchewan.

Above: A ballast spreader.

A siding in Brandon, Manitoba.

Left: After crossing the Prairies, a railway car arrives in Calgary encrusted with snow.

Below: The Canadian in Brandon, Manitoba.

Opposite top: The Canadian in Regina, Saskatchewan.

Opposite bottom: A cold winter morning in Calgary.

Top left: The oldest operating steam locomotive in Canada sits on a siding at the CN station in Winnipeg. One of thirty manufactured in Glasgow, Scotland, for Canadian Pacific in 1882, it now belongs to a vintage-locomotive society in Winnipeg, which operates a tourist railway called the Prairie Dog Central.

Middle left: Close-up of the locomotive's cylinder and front trunk.

Bottom left: Overlapping view of CN freight car, vintage locomotive and vintage coach.

Above: The CPR's Lethbridge Viaduct, completed in 1909, is the highest railway bridge in Canada. Spanning the Oldman River in Alberta, it is 5,328 feet long and 314 feet high.

South of Winnipeg, the CPR line crosses
the Trans-Canada Highway.

Stockyards in St. Boniface, Manitoba. Now that trucking companies have largely taken over the business of transporting cattle, rail stockyards are rarely used.

Overleaf: A prairie landscape in southwestern Saskatchewan.

Railway station in Medicine Hat, Alberta. According to legend, Medicine Hat derived its name from a skirmish between Cree and Blackfoot Indians. When a gust of wind blew the hat of the Cree medicine man into the Saskatchewan River, the Cree, fearing it was an unlucky omen, fled. The site became known as "the place where the medicine man lost his hat," later contracted to Medicine Hat.

The CPR's Number 14A station, built in southern Saskatchewan during the 1930s, has been converted into a farmhouse. The freight door now opens into a garage. A maze of branch lines sprouted across southern Saskatchewan and Alberta in the first few decades of this century. Many are now abandoned, and once-thriving stations have become ghost towns.

THE MOUNTAINS

Above: Surveyors charting the railway's path through the Kicking Horse Canyon in British Columbia (*c.* 1880).

Left: The westbound Canadian passes through the Rockies near Field, British Columbia.

In the Rockies, the real show begins, the wide-screen epic that lures tourists from all over the world. Travel posters have already made many visitors familiar with the star performers, the young and muscular mountains that are not as high as the Himalayas nor as elegant as the Alps, but which shudder with a kinetic energy that seems only a thrust removed from the geological upheavals that created them.

For an hour, the foothills west of Calgary served as a suspenseful overture and were a welcome relief after the linear monotony of the Prairies. The audience took their seats in the dome cars, cameras ready. The sky was clear. As we made our way along the broad bank of the Bow River, mountains appeared on either side, turning the Bow Valley into a grand hallway—entrance to the Canadian Louvre, Banff National Park.

Banff, the park's postcard-perfect capital, is unlike any other community in the country. Surrounded by mountains suitable for framing, the town, with its hot-sulphur springs and exotic shops, is a total confection for tourists. The Banff Springs Hotel, rising out of a secluded valley with almost absurd majesty, is a true castle. It is the pride of the CP chain and the one hotel fully worthy of the name château both inside and out. Its baronial halls are lined with antique oak desks and cabinets that seem to serve little purpose other than keeping an army of young employees busy dusting and polishing. Its windows command such devastating views that the architects (perhaps disoriented) designed the hotel facing away from the mountains. CPR manager William Van Horne stepped in at the last moment and sketched in a rotunda to disguise the error. Once the hotel attracted aristocrats who would arrive on trains from cities such as Chicago and St. Paul to "take the waters." Now tour groups of Japanese form its most regular clientele.

At Banff, I moved from the dome car to the locomotive cab, the best vantage point for the ride through the mountain passes and canyons ahead. The initial thirty-five-mile stretch of the Bow Valley leading to Lake Louise was like an open zoo. We were hardly out of the Banff station before a bushy-tailed coyote was sprinting down the track in front of us. A couple of whistle blasts eventually sent him scampering down the embankment and into the woods. Farther on, beside the track, more coyotes and a flock of ravens scattered as we passed. They had been devouring the bloody carcass of an elk killed by a previous train. Snow forces elk down from the high country, and each winter trains kill about a hundred.

"That's why there are so many coyotes down here," explained the second engineer. "They thrive on dead elk. But it's good we kill so many, because they tend to get overpopulated and starve."

Under the ocher bluffs of Castle Mountain, which looks as if it might well have been the architectural inspiration for the château hotels, we passed a large herd of elk spread along both sides of the track, some standing, some sitting in the snow, none (thankfully) on the track.

We made a brief stop at the log station in Lake Louise, where yet another CP château, a poor cousin to the Banff Springs, presides over one of the most symmetrical slices of scenery in the world. We then left the broad corridor of the Bow Valley and headed into the mountains toward barriers that, before the CPR, everyone had assumed were insurmountable.

A stone cairn marks the Continental Divide. At a mile above sea level, it is the highest point on the whole line. Near the track a stream splits into two branches, one flowing east toward Hudson Bay, the other west to the Pacific Ocean. The divide itself is unspectacular; the excitement began as we made our descent of the Kicking Horse Pass through the famous Spiral Tunnels.

Before the CPR drilled the tunnels in 1909, trains had to negotiate a 4.4 percent grade as they made their way down the western side of the pass. Known as the Big Hill, it was steeper than any stretch of consistently used standard-gauge track in the world, and despite some fatal mishaps, it carried trains for twenty-five years until the Spiral Tunnels were completed. The geometry of the tunnels is confusing for the passenger. The train carves a 288-degree turn through the upper tunnel, then a 226-degree loop through the lower tunnel. In each tunnel, the track crosses over itself. Their combined lengths total 6,177 feet. With a long freight train, as the locomotive exits from the bottom portal of the lower tunnel, its tail end can be seen rattling overhead on its way into the upper portal. Together, the tunnels form a figure eight, and they tend to throw the most stubborn sense of direction off kilter.

Passing through the Spirals felt like going down a mine shaft. The beam from the locomotive's headlamp glanced off roughhewn walls that dripped with icicles. Halfway through the first tunnel, the engineer switched off the light for a moment to give me a scare.

At the bottom of the Big Hill is the town of Field, which was a bustling rail center in the age of steam, when extra locomotives were needed to push trains up the grade. Today it is a village but trains still change crews there. Our new engineer was a gregarious forty-three-year veteran named G. H. Popplewell, who liked to be called Pop.

We followed the downward route of the turbulent Kicking Horse River; the track wound along the rim of steep gorges

Passengers on the Grand Trunk Pacific line at Moose Lake, Alberta, in 1915. Taking a northern route through the Rockies via Jasper and the Yellowhead Pass, the GTP later became part of the Canadian National.

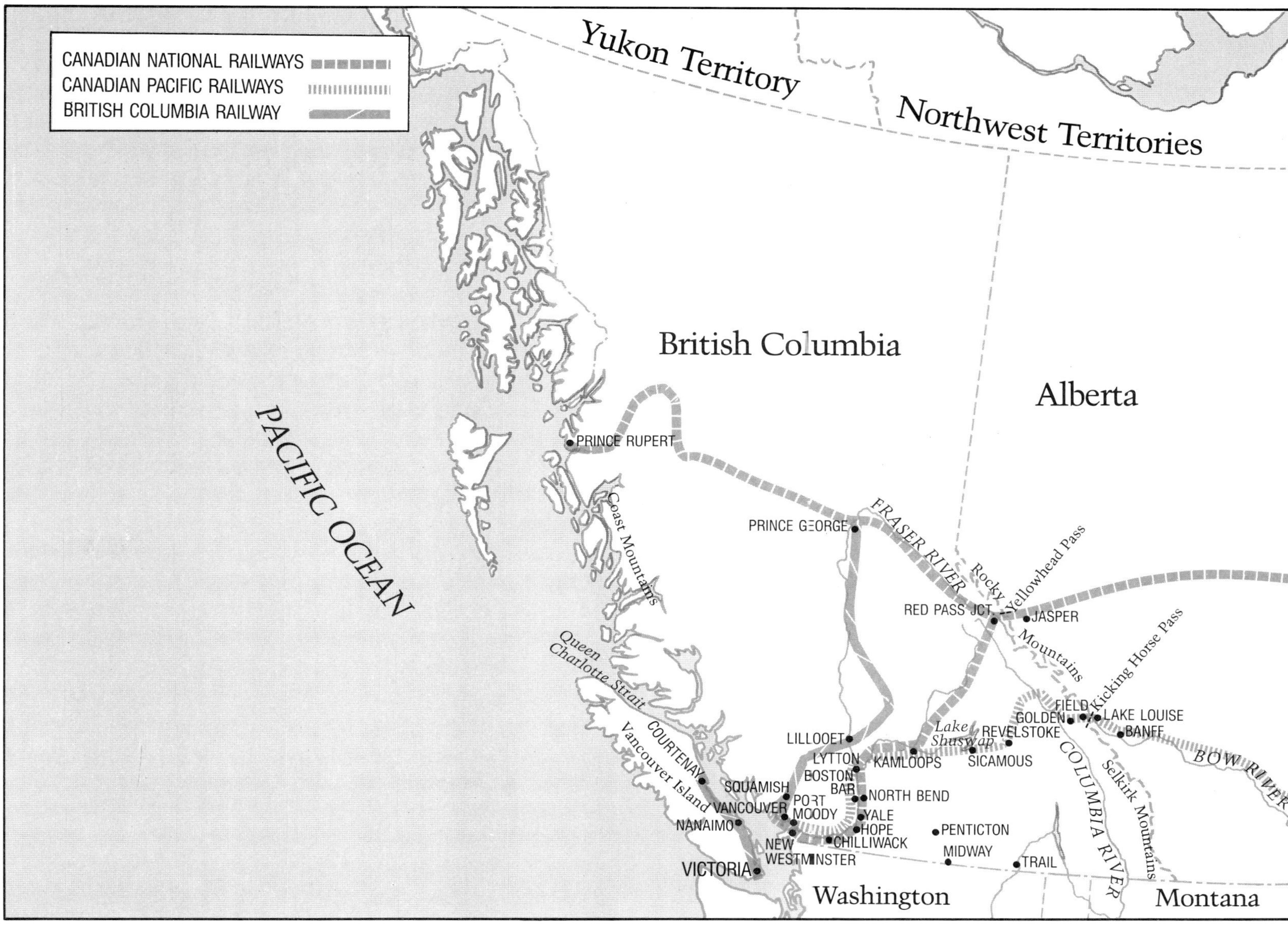

and crisscrossed the river half a dozen times. Pop reminisced about the glory days of driving an oil-fired 5900, "with white steam puffing out the exhaust, just crackin' in the cold air." The track clung to the wall of the Kicking Horse Canyon past sheer cliffs of twisted shale, the water a white-green torrent below. "Our last 5900 upset and landed in the river," said Pop, pointing to the exact spot. "Our fireman fell out and landed on that rock over there. He was all right, but the hogger [engineer] was killed." Farther along, he showed me a curve where he derailed in 1966 after slamming into a rock the height of a kitchen table.

The track drops 1,489 feet in the 34-mile stretch from Field to Golden, where the Kicking Horse River joins the Columbia, which provides hydroelectricity for most of the province and flows for a distance of 1,550 miles. We followed its broad, fertile valley until it narrowed into another canyon laced with waterfalls. Ahead lay the Selkirks, the range that crested the original spine of the North American continent, mountains that were old before the Rockies were born. We had caught glimpses of them earlier along the route—jagged rows of incisors, enameled with glaciers. Far more barren and inhospitable than the Rockies, they formed a barrier that the CPR's original engineers had feared was impenetrable.

The surveyor who first explored the CPR's route through the mountains was Major A. B. Rogers, an Indian fighter from the American midwest who had never seen a mountain until the railway hired him in 1881. A tough old codger with a mass of white whiskers, Rogers became known for his ability to live on nothing but chewing tobacco and beans for weeks on end. He fought his way through dense brush, scaled gorges swollen with glacier-fed torrents and trekked through snowfields in repeated attempts to find a pass through the Selkirks. He was driven by a single burning ambition — to achieve immortality by getting his name on the map. On July 24, 1882, he achieved his goal by discovering the route through what is now known as the Rogers Pass.

But the route was fraught with problems. During the winter, snowfalls of up to fifty feet at the summit of the pass made tracklaying a nightmare. Snowslides, generating their own cyclones, would decimate forests and destroy anything in their path. Sometimes builders cut the roadbed directly through the debris; one cut was known as the Plum Pudding Cut because the shorn-off trees looked like raisins in a cake.

Once the railway was operating, avalanches kept wiping out large sections of it in the pass, and between 1885 and 1909, two hundred men died working to maintain the track. In 1910, a single snowslide killed another sixty-two men. Subsequently, as part of a plan to double-track the transcontinental main line, the CPR gave up on the Rogers Pass and drilled a tunnel 540 feet below it. Completed in 1916, the Connaught Tunnel was the longest double-tracked tunnel on the continent. Later it was converted to single track to accommodate larger freight loads.

Looking west from the hotel in Field, British Columbia, in 1887.

Now the CPR is boring another tunnel below it to reduce the grade by 500 feet. When completed in 1989, with a length of 9.1 miles, it will be the longest main-line tunnel in the western hemisphere.

The Selkirks section of the CPR line is the busiest single-track rail line in North America; it handles as many as thirty-four trains a day. As we began climbing the eastern slopes via the Beaver River Valley, we passed a typical freight load. Lined up on a siding at a "pusher" terminal, 110 coal cars were waiting to ascend the grade. The 14,000–ton dead weight was coupled to four locomotives at the head end, six "pusher" engines on the rear and two "slaves" in the middle—twelve units with a combined muscle of 36,000 horsepower. The coal was bound for the west coast. There, a ship would carry it to Japan, where it would heat blast furnaces to forge steel to make automobiles that would be ferried across the Pacific and loaded on trains and hauled across this same stretch of track to Canadian car buyers.

The track took us along a mountain ledge flanked by massive cedars and firs. Even in November the trees were already laden with snow. Higher up, we could see the old Rogers Pass route, now paved over by the Trans-Canada Highway. We crossed ravines and gorges over a variety of slender supports, such as the Surprise Creek Bridge, which spans a 170-foot gulch where one can still see wreckage from a previous bridge that collapsed under the weight of two steam locomotives in 1929. And the Stoney Creek Bridge, the highest on the entire line, is a miracle of curved steel — two arches stuck like a spider's web to the walls of a 325-foot chasm.

The Surprise Creek Bridge in British Columbia's Selkirk Mountains (*c.* 1895). Visible are both the original timber trestle and the steel arch structure that replaced it. In 1929, as a third bridge was being built to handle heavier loads, the steel arch collapsed under the weight of two steam locomotives. One reached the other side, but the second engine plunged 170 feet into the gorge, killing two men.

As we approached Connaught Tunnel, the locomotive appeared to be on a collision course with a mountain. In the middle was a small mouse hole, growing larger. The train aimed for the mouse hole and disappeared.

At Revelstoke, I moved back to the passenger section and had dinner with a potato-chip salesman from the town of Golden, who convinced me he had the perfect life. He spent his workdays driving a potato-chip truck around Banff and Lake Louise; in his spare time, he went hunting and fishing, bringing home enough deer, elk, moose and salmon to keep his freezer well-stocked year-round. Rejecting modern weapons as unfair, he used only a bow and arrow or a homemade flintlock and black powder. He advised me that elk was the best of the game meats: "You can slice it with a fork."

At the next table, oddly enough, was another potato-chip salesman from the American head office of a rival company. He was traveling with a pretzel man and a peanut man. The three of them formed a sales delegation from a snack-food empire who were making their annual swing through western Canada by rail. The pretzel man did all the talking, even on the subject of his firm's potato chips, which he loudly proclaimed were the best on earth. The flintlock-loving chip man from Golden did not rise to the provocation. He was not terribly serious about chips. For him, they were only a means to an end.

It was our last night on the train, and after dinner we all assembled in the lounge car for drinks: the English globe-trotter, the American tourists, the potato chippers and some new passengers who got on in Calgary, including a Vancouver music promoter wearing a pair of contraband lizard-skin boots that he inherited from a friend who died when he fell asleep behind the wheel of his car in a tunnel. Trains bring together the most unlikely drinking companions.

In the dark, the Canadian traversed more mountain ranges and passed the stone cairn that commemorates the spot where the CPR's last spike was hammered in on November 7, 1885. "A nebulous dream was a reality," reads a nearby plaque. "An iron ribbon crossed Canada from sea to sea." Descending beside the Eagle River and then rounding the shoreline of Lake Shuswap, the train headed for the Pacific by tracing the same 315-mile route followed by some two million sockeye salmon each October — the Thompson and Fraser rivers.

The track that winds along the Fraser Canyon is one of the most dangerous sections of railway in the country. Mountains of granite veined with hard quartz flank both sides of the river, rising up to eight thousand feet. Both the CP and CN transcontinental lines run through the canyon, one on either wall. The construction of the original CP line, which began in 1880, was more costly — in dollars and lives — than any comparable length of track in Canada. The government subcontracted the work to an American named Andrew Onderdonk, who had built the first subway tunnels under New York's East River. Onderdonk's men spent the first eighteen months simply blasting and drilling rock along a two-mile strip of the sixty-mile canyon without laying a single rail. The first thirteen miles north of their base at Yale required seventeen tunnels, and a single thirty-mile section of the chasm required one hundred wooden bridges and trestles.

It was difficult to find men willing to undertake such perilous work. Indians suspended by ropes would drill holes for explosives in the rock face. But for the bulk of his labor force, Onderdonk hired Chinese coolies at a dollar a day. He first brought them in via the United States, and then in 1882 he imported six thousand Chinese in ten shiploads directly from Hong Kong. Without this pool of cheap immigrant labor, Onderdonk's operation would have collapsed. In places where mules were unavailable, Chinese were sometimes used as beasts of burden to haul wagons. They were seen as more expendable than whites, and casualty rates along the Fraser, though not scrupulously recorded, were enormous. Deaths occurred almost weekly.

The Canadian descended the canyon in the dead of night, but from my roomette window the gothic crags were eerily visible in the moonlight. Downstream from the canyon, the river gradually widened into the marshy pastureland of the Fraser Delta. By dawn we were in Vancouver.

Appropriately, Canada's third largest city (population: 1.3 million) originated as yet another creation of the CPR. As late as 1884, everyone had assumed the line's Pacific terminus would be Port Moody, at the head of Burrard Inlet. But, despite the frenzy of speculation and construction going on in that fledgling town, Van Horne decided it lacked the space for a major

Donald A. Smith, a director of the CPR, drives the last spike at Craigellachie, British Columbia, on November 7, 1885. Standing directly behind him with his hands in his pockets is William Van Horne, the CPR general manager who oversaw the building of the transcontinental line. Standing between Smith and Van Horne is Sir Sandford Fleming, who conducted the first surveys for a route to the Pacific.

Building the railway along the walls of the Fraser Canyon between Yale and Boston Bar in 1881. In the foreground is the first of seventeen tunnels blasted in a thirteen-mile stretch north of Yale.

A Chinese work gang on the CPR line just west of the Rogers Pass in 1889. Some ten thousand Chinese were imported to help drive the railway through the mountains in the early 1880s.

city. Instead, he opted for English Bay, where Vancouver now lies between the mountains and the sea, occupying the most idyllic setting of any city in Canada.

I was surprised that after traveling across the country on the train I had no desire to get off. I had become attached to its reassuring rhythms and its eccentric society — an inner world that instantly dissolved as the passengers dispersed into the stone-lined vault of the station. I took a cab to CN's Hotel Vancouver, a massive yet gracious hotel with a green château roof and stone gargoyles.

At dawn the next day I was on another train, heading north on the British Columbia Railway. It shuffled up the indented shoreline of Howe Sound across from blue-green mountains swathed in Oriental mists, climbed the Coast Range through trees that turned from green to white until they were clotted with snow, shimmied down the other side, skirted a long, fiordlike lake walled with mountains rising from jade waters. . . . It was a one-day outing, but on the BCR, which stretches north to the Alaska Highway, you feel you could ride to the ends of the earth.

For one final excursion, I left the continental mainland. The journey would end as it began — on an island. Just as Newfoundland punctuates Canada's Atlantic coast, Vancouver Island punctuates its Pacific coast. But the two islands have little in common. Although both are carpeted with forests, Newfoundland has modest evergreens, while Vancouver Island boasts some of the most impressive stands of cedar, hemlock and Douglas fir anywhere. Their main ports, St. John's and Victoria, are both steeped in British tradition, but the colonial charm of St. John's was created by ale-swilling pirates and fishermen, while Victoria's crystal-palace integrity belongs to the imperial gentry.

The Malahat Dayliner travels 140 miles from Victoria to Courtenay along a line that originated as the Esquimalt and Nanaimo Railway, built in 1884 by coal baron Robert Dunsmuir to service his mines. I intercepted the Dayliner at Nanaimo and continued to the end of the line then rode it back to Victoria. I soon realized it was no ordinary train ride. Many of the stations were antique, lovingly restored, and on display at various points along the route were polished steam engines, old cabooses with fresh coats of orange paint and modern murals depicting pioneers and Indians. Historical brochures hung from hooks above the coach seats, and the conductor behaved like a cross between a curator and a maitre d'.

It was raining as we headed south from Courtenay, past a lumberyard where massive timbers, stripped bare and shining wet, were stacked as smooth and straight as sewer pipes. Much of the line is flanked with forests, and dead trees are constantly falling on the track. (The engineer never travels without a chain saw.) We crossed numerous rivers, though none as remarkable as a creek north of Nanaimo. It was teeming with salmon swimming upstream to spawn—so many that there appeared to be more fish than water. They began wriggling back downstream as the train hit the bridge. "They scare real easy," said the engineer. He slowed the engine to a crawl and the fish resumed their original pattern, like iron filings drawn to a magnet. Farther on, as we rounded Nanoose Bay, the conductor pointed out a yellow submarine floating offshore. I blinked. The bay is a testing area for underwater weapons. The military once tried training beluga whales to retrieve torpedoes there, but environmentalists put a stop to it.

South of Nanaimo, we passed through an English countryside of emerald pastures and old farmhouses. The conductor seemed to know most of the occupants: "There was one old guy in his eighties. We used to pick him up at his front door. They won't let us do that any more. We're only allowed to stop at stations." As we approached Victoria, the conductor was waving to people every minute or so—all regulars. He pointed to a little girl and her mother silhouetted by a bedroom light. "The girl has been waving to us ever since she could move her arm," he said. "They were on the train one time, and we didn't even know it was them. They told us who they were just as they were getting off. It's sad because if we'd known, we could have given them a proper tour."

It was dark as we entered Victoria. The provincial parliament was lit up like a midway pavilion, and beside it stood the last of the CP hotels, the gothic dowager known as the Empress. Before I disembarked, the conductor asked me to make an entry in "the log." I had traveled more than four thousand miles across Canada, but it was the first time I had traveled on a train with a guest book.

A load of timber leaves Hastings Mill in Vancouver (*c.* 1890).

Right: An eastbound freight churns through the snow-covered Bow Valley.

5820
5820

Top: A freight locomotive and a Budd car in the roundhouse in Victoria, British Columbia.

Bottom: Bridge over the Fraser River at Chilliwack, British Columbia.

Right: Budd car dayliner in Victoria's roundhouse.

Overleaf: The westbound Canadian near the Spiral Tunnels.

VIA

The station at Midway, British Columbia.

The Canadian, leaving Field, British Columbia, heading west.

Previous pages: The Banff Springs Hotel in Banff National Park. Surrounded by Canada's most famous scenery, the hotel is the flagship of the Canadian Pacific chain. It once catered to American aristocrats, who would come by train to "take the waters" at Banff's sulphur springs. Today, many of the guests come on tour-package flights from Japan.

Above: Riding the British Columbia Railway up the shoreline of Howe Sound in the early morning. The third largest railway in Canada, BC Rail operates 1,260 miles of track. Its routes extend like a steel spine to the northern extremes of the province and cut through some of the most spectacular mountain scenery on the continent.

The CPR station at Boston Bar on the Fraser River. A unique cable car links Boston Bar to the community of North Bend, on the opposite side of the river. Carrying one automobile at a time, it glides 120 feet above the water, but at flood time that distance may shrink to thirty feet.

Overleaf: The British Columbia Railway snakes along the shore of Howe Sound near the logging town of Squamish. The Cariboo Dayliner continues another 428 miles north to Prince George.

The CPR and CNR cross the Fraser Canyon on separate bridges at Siska Flat. The CPR bridge is in the foreground. Cutting the original CPR roadbed through the canyon was a difficult and hazardous operation that took four years of intense work. With a lot of dynamite and the help of about ten thousand laborers imported from China, American subcontractor Andrew Onderdonk completed this section of the CPR in 1884. During the construction, casualties occurred regularly.

A CNR freight crosses the Thompson River near Lytton, British Columbia.

Left: The CNR line along the Fraser River viewed from Mule Mountain.

Above: A ferry from Vancouver Island arrives at Horseshoe Bay in West Vancouver.

The CP Rail grain terminal and the Second Narrows Bridge in Vancouver. About five million tons of prairie grain are shipped out of Vancouver each year.

A freight yard in Victoria, terminal of the Vancouver Island line that started out as the Esquimalt and Nanaimo Railway in 1884. Coal baron Robert Dunsmuir built it to serve his mines and the CPR bought it in 1905. Today, Vancouver Island also has a considerable network of private logging railways.

Overleaf: British Columbia Railway's Cariboo Dayliner winds along the edge of the Cheakamus Canyon in the Coast Range. As the train traces the course of the Cheakamus River through the range, it climbs to an altitude of 2,200 feet.

THE EMPRESS

Left: The most westerly link in Canadian Pacific's hotel chain, the Empress. A bastion of Victoria's British gentry, it is famous for its afternoon ritual of crumpets and tea.

Above: Log booms off Vancouver Island near Chemainus. Trees are British Columbia's most important resource, and with logging operations threatening the last magnificent stands of virgin timber on the coastal islands, there have been bitter conflicts between environmentalists and the lumber industry.

The Malahat Dayliner, which consists of two self-propelled Budd cars, travels through the verdant landscape of Vancouver Island.

Right: Vancouver's last operational steam locomotive—a two-truck Lima Shay locomotive (Number 3147) built in 1920—takes a tour through grounds of Cowichan Valley Forest Museum at Duncan.

The Canadian leaves Vancouver, heading east.

A GUIDE TO CANADA'S RAILWAYS

THE LINES

Canada's first railway was the **Champlain and St. Lawrence Railroad**, a 14-mile line that opened in 1836. It ran from the town of St. Jean on the Richelieu River north to the St. Lawrence River near Montreal. The rails were wood with strips of iron nailed on top. By 1850, only six lines, with a total length of 80 miles, existed in what was then known as British North America; three of them were short bypasses skirting obstructions in water routes. With government help, there was a construction boom from 1850 to 1860, and by the birth of Canadian Confederation, on July 1, 1867, the country had fifteen railways totaling 2,495 miles, 485 locomotives, 684 passenger cars and 4,214 freight cars. Until 1870, 90 percent of the track was broad gauge (5 feet, 6 inches).

The **Grand Trunk Railway**, incorporated in 1852, connected Montreal to Portland, Maine. It completed the first line between Montreal and Toronto in 1856. Buying up smaller lines, the GTR had 3,000 miles of track by the turn of the century. Supported by British capital, it acquired U.S. lines, which became part of the **Grand Trunk Western Railway**, and built the **Grand Trunk Pacific** in the west. All the Grand Trunk lines were absorbed by the government's Canadian National in 1923.

The **Great Western Railway** was officially formed in 1834 but did not blossom until the 1850s. By 1858 it operated 360 miles of track that linked Toronto, Windsor, Sarnia and Niagara Falls. It was taken over by the Grand Trunk in 1882.

The **Nova Scotia Railway** was built from Halifax to Truro and Windsor in the 1850s. It had iron rails that were the same shape on the top and bottom; when they became worn they could be turned upside down.

The **Intercolonial Railway**, which opened in 1876, linked Nova Scotia and New Brunswick to Quebec. Its iron bridges and steel rails were considered state-of-the-art features at the time. The ICR was built to fulfill a Confederation pledge and included the narrow-gauge **Prince Edward Island Railway**. The ICR's 1,800 miles of track were absorbed by Canadian National.

Canadian Pacific completed the first transcontinental road in 1885 — a 2,900-mile line that was the largest rail network in the world at the time.

The **Canadian Northern Railway**, founded in 1896, completed a line to Vancouver in 1915. By 1918, when it was taken over by Canadian National, it had 9,433 miles of track, more than any line in the country.

The **Grand Trunk Pacific Railway**, launched in 1905, extended a line through Edmonton and the Rockies to the Pacific port of Prince Rupert, 550 miles north of Vancouver. Its chief promoter, Charles Hays, died on the *Titanic*'s ill-fated maiden voyage in 1912, two years before the line opened. The GTPR was built in tandem with the government's **National Transcontinental Railway**, which took a northern route from Moncton to Winnipeg.

Canadian National Railways, created by the government in 1919, owned 22,096 miles of track by 1923. It absorbed 221 railway companies, including all trunk lines except the CPR.

The **Hudson Bay Railway** was born in 1886, but track did not reach the polar-bear port of Churchill until 1929. It joined Canadian National in 1951.

The **Algoma Central Railway**, an Ontario line from Sault Ste. Marie to Hearst, fell short of its original plan to reach Hudson Bay. Construction began in 1911 and ended in 1914.

The **Ontario Northland Railway** evolved from the **Temiskaming and Northern Ontario Railway**. Construction began in 1902, and the line followed the mining boom north. It reached the shores of James Bay in 1932.

The **British Columbia Railway** is a provincial line that started out as the **Pacific Great Eastern** in 1912. The line did not reach Prince George until 1952. Today it is Canada's third-largest railway, and its track, extending to Fort Nelson, forms a steel spine through the mountains of British Columbia.

The **Quebec North Shore and Labrador Line** links the Quebec port of Sept Iles with the mining town of Shefferville, 365 miles to the north in Labrador. It was built between 1950 and 1954. It once carried 260-car trains loaded with iron ore. The mines were shut down in 1982.

Distances covered by Canada's major contemporary lines:

Canadian National Railways	32,000 miles
Canadian Pacific Railways	21,500 miles
British Columbia Railway	1,260 miles
Ontario Northland Railway	570 miles
Quebec North Shore and Labrador Line	394 miles
Algoma Central Railway	296 miles

TUNNELS AND BRIDGES

Canada's two major railways have a combined total of 157 tunnels and 9,239 bridges. The CNR has 72 tunnels, with a combined length of 14.7 miles, and 5,699 bridges, totaling 145 miles. The CPR has 85 tunnels, with a combined length of 15 miles, and 3,540 bridges, totaling 85 miles.

The longest main-line railway tunnel in Canada is the 5.6-mile Table Tunnel on the British Columbia Railway's branch line to the Tumbler Ridge coalfields in northwest British Columbia. It burrows through the Rocky Mountains 1,800 feet below the peak of Table Mountain. Drilling began in April 1982, and the tunnel was completed in August 1983. The branch line also has Canada's third-longest tunnel, the 3.8-mile Wolverine Tunnel.

Canada's second-longest tunnel, and the longest one to carry main-line passenger trains, is Canadian Pacific's Connaught Tunnel, boring 5 miles, 39 yards through Mt. Macdonald, a 9,483-foot peak in the Selkirks. Opened on December 6, 1916, the tunnel replaced the Rogers Pass route, which was often blocked by snow in winter despite 4 miles of snowsheds. The tunnel lowered the route's summit by 540 feet, shortened the route by 4.5 miles and eliminated curves that made seven complete circles. Originally the longest double-tracked tunnel in North America, it was converted to single track in 1959 to accommodate higher loads.

The original Stoney Creek Bridge in 1887.

A new CPR tunnel through Mt. Macdonald should be completed by 1989. With a length of 9.1 miles, it will be the longest tunnel in the Western hemisphere. It will lower the grade by 500 feet. A unique ventilation system will allow heavy freight traffic. As a train approaches the east portal, a door will open automatically; another door in the middle of the tunnel will remain closed until the train reaches it. Fresh air will be pumped into the eastern half of the tunnel. As the train travels through the western half, it will be ventilated, as the mid-tunnel door will be closed again.

The longest tunnel on Canadian National's line is Mount Royal Tunnel — 3 miles, 288 yards long. The Canadian Northern Railway built it between 1912 and 1914 to bring trains into downtown Montreal, to compete with CP and the Grand Trunk. The first passengers to pass through it, on October 21, 1918, were pulled by an electric locomotive, which is still in use on a 17-mile commuter run to Deux Montagnes.

The Spiral Tunnels, completed in 1919, were modeled after those in Switzerland's St. Gotthard Pass. They replaced a 4.4-percent grade on Big Hill, in the Kicking Horse Pass. A train entering the upper tunnel carves a 288-degree loop through Cathedral Mountain over a distance of 3,255 feet before emerging 56 feet below. It then enters the lower tunnel, which burrows 2,922 feet through Mt. Ogden, making a 226-degree loop before emerging 45 feet below. Together the tunnels form a figure eight.

The longest railway bridge in Canada is the Victoria Bridge, which carries the CNR over the St. Lawrence River in Montreal. It has 24 piers and 25 spans. The ironwork is 6,592 feet long; including approaches the bridge is 9,145 feet long. The original bridge, a single-track enclosed tubular structure, opened in 1859. In 1898 it was replaced by a double-track bridge of steel superstructure, which has been modified several times.

The highest railway bridge in Canada is the Lethbridge Viaduct, which carries the CPR over the Oldman River in Alberta. It has 34 spans on steel towers. It is 5,328 feet long, 314 feet high and dead straight. Completed in 1909, it consumed 12,000 tons of steel. It is the longest bridge on the CPR system.

The longest cantilever span in the world belongs to the Quebec Bridge, which crosses the St. Lawrence River at Quebec City. Now owned by the CNR, the bridge was completed in 1917 after two serious construction accidents that claimed 86 lives. It is 3,238 feet long and 150 feet high. The center span is 1,800 feet between the piers.

The second-highest bridge in Canada is the British Columbia Railway's Deep Creek Bridge, 331 miles north of Vancouver. It is 312 feet high and opened in 1921.

The Stoney Creek Bridge rises 307 feet from a gorge east of the Connaught Tunnel on the CPR line. Originally built in 1886 as a timber Howe-truss deck-type bridge supported on timber towers, it was the highest wooden bridge in the world. In 1893–94 it was replaced by a steel-arch span of 336 feet, which was the world's only parallel double-chorded arch with its main hinge pins in its lower chord. In 1929 the bridge was reinforced by new deck girders and additional arches and supports.

The highest bridge on the CNR carries its main transcontinental line over the Pembina River west of Edmonton, Alberta. A steel trestle structure, it is 213 feet high and 900 feet long.

MOTIVE POWER

The first steam engine in British North America was the six-ton **Dorchester**, built by Robert Stephenson and Company, Newcastle-on-Tyne, in 1835, and put into service on the pioneer Champlain and St. Lawrence Railroad on July 21, 1836. It was not an experiment but a regular production locomotive — the 127th produced by the Stephenson works. It was only thirteen feet long but had a very high smokestack to prevent sparks from setting fire to trees and grass alongside the track.

A season's experience proved the locomotive to be too small and a second one, delivered in 1837, was a United States product, the **Jason C. Pierce**. Built by William Norris in Philadelphia, it was a locomotive with a 4-2-0 wheel arrangement. Both locomotives were subsequently rebuilt and had long careers. The Dorchester lasted until 1864, the Pierce until 1887.

The first locomotive built in Canada was the **Toronto**, constructed in the city of Toronto in 1853 by James Good for the Ontario, Simcoe and Huron Union Rail Road. Before the end of the decade, locomotive-building establishments had opened in Montreal, Kingston and Hamilton.

The first distinctive group of locomotives built for use in Canada were sixty engines built by Peto, Brassey, Betts and Jackson at their works in Birkenhead, near Liverpool, England. PBB&J had contracts to build major sections of the Grand Trunk Railway and the Birkenhead works were built to produce motive power and rolling stock. They were, in fact, called the "Canada Works." The Birkenhead locomotives were successful in design, but because they were built to the broad gauge of 66 inches, most were retired in the 1870s. (Transforming them to standard gauge would have been expensive.) One, however, remained in service on the portage railway at Carillon until 1910.

The 4-4-0 wheel arrangement was the most common type used in North America between 1850 and 1890. The 4-4-0 locomotive became known as the "American Standard" or the "Standard." With driving wheels of various sizes, it could be adapted to the whole spectrum of railway requirements. Engines in freight and yard service usually had smaller driving wheels, 56 inches to 63 inches in diameter. Passenger trains had wheel diameters of 69 inches to 75 inches.

In the 1880s a heavier locomotive with an extra set of driving wheels, the 4-6-0, was manufactured. It became the most well-known locomotive in the CPR fleet. Between 1905 and 1913, 502 4-6-0s of the D-10 class were built for the CPR, 119 in the company's own Angus shops, 265 by Montreal Locomotive Works (MLW), 68 by the Canadian Locomotive Company (CLC) in Kingston and 50 by United States firms. Members of this class survived on the CPR roster right up to 1960, when the railway stopped using steam.

After the turn of the century, technological advances such as superheating brought newer and larger locomotives into use. They included the 4-6-2 (**Pacific** type), which began hauling passenger trains on the Intercolonial Railway in 1905, and the 4-8-4 (**Northern** type), which became the backbone of the CNR fleet. In June 1927, just six months after the Northern Pacific Railroad in the United States introduced the 4-8-4 design, CN received its first 4-8-4, the 6100, from the CLC. It was the prototype of a CN 4-8-4 fleet that eventually totaled 203 locomotives, the largest ownership anywhere. CN's Northern locomotive (series 6100s, 6200s and 6300s) handled 16-car passenger trains or 80-car freights with ease. Its maximum horsepower was 2,900 horsepower. In 1925 CN introduced the **Mountain** type, a 4-8-2 that was 90 feet long and 20 percent more powerful than the largest engine then in service in Canada.

A classic Canadian steam locomotive is the 4-6-4 **Hudson** type, which first appeared on CP lines in 1929 and 1930 when 20 units were built for heavy passenger services requiring

Manufactured in 1883, this steam engine (with the Standard 4-4-0 wheel arrangement) was the first locomotive built by the CPR's own shops in Montreal.

A Pacific-type steam locomotive (with a 4-6-2 wheel arrangement), class G5, built by the CPR's Angus shops in Montreal in 1944. The photograph was taken at the Angus shops in 1967 before the locomotive was delivered to the National Museum of Science and Technology in Ottawa.

reasonably high speeds. These original units were not streamlined, but the remaining 45 units built during and after 1937 incorporated the distinctive Canadian Pacific streamlining in their design. One of them, No. 2850, was selected to haul the 1939 royal train, which carried King George and Queen Elizabeth 3,100 miles across Canada. Never before had a train completed such a long run on the North American continent without a change in engine. The locomotive's standard tuscan-red paint scheme was refinished in royal blue and aluminum with a royal crown at the front of each running board. Subsequently, all 45 semi-streamlined 4-6-4s were adorned with crowns and became known as Royal Hudsons. A number of Royal Hudsons have been preserved, notably the original, No. 2850.

In the 1930s, the largest and heaviest steam locomotives in the continent were Canadian Pacific's 5900 series of 2-10-4 **Selkirk** types. Known as Texas types in the United States, the 36 Canadian models were named after British Columbia's Selkirk range, where they were in daily operation. Like the Hudsons, they were built at the Montreal Locomotive Works. The last standard-gauge steam engine built for a Canadian railway, No. 5935, is on display at the Canadian Railway Museum in Montreal. It was retired from service only sixteen years after it was built.

The first successful road diesel locomotive in North America was built for the CNR in 1928. The first two units to form the No. 9000 series came from the CLC in 1928. Together they were rated at 50 percent, the same as a Mountain 4-8-2. Black with gold lettering, they were used as two coupled units until 1939. During the Second World War, the original No. 9000 formed part of a seven-car No. 1 Armoured Train, used to protect some 80 miles of track along the Skeena River between Prince Rupert and the interior.

The CPR first used diesel in 1937, when a 600-horsepower diesel-electric switching locomotive was placed in service as an experiment. The company acquired its first diesel electrics for road service in 1948 and 1949; they ranged from 1,000 horsepower to 2,250 horsepower. Both CN and CP carried out a wholesale conversion from steam to diesel power during the 1950s.

A standard unit in use on Canada's railways today is a 3,000-horsepower freight locomotive built by General Motors Diesel Limited of London, Ontario. Passenger services use 1,800-horsepower diesel electrics manufactured by GM and Montreal Locomotive Works. Their maximum speed is 89 miles per hour. The country's newest locomotives are the 2,700-horsepower LRC diesel electrics manufactured by MLW.

The CNR owns a fleet of about 2,200 diesel electrics, the CPR 1,200, and the VIA passenger service 145.

PASSENGER CARS

One of the world's first sleeping cars was designed and built in Hamilton, Ontario, in 1857 by the Great Western Railway. The GWR also introduced Canada's first postal car with a letter-sorting facility (1854), its first parlor cars (1860) and its first diners (1876). In 1870, the Grand Trunk Railroad built Pullman Palace cars at its shops in Montreal.

The first self-propelled passenger cars in Canada were built by Canadian General Electric for the Canadian Northern Railway in 1912. By 1926, Canadian National had 36 self-propelled cars. (In the 1950s and 1960s they were replaced by RDCs from the Budd Company of Philadelphia, which are still in use on short interurban runs.)

During the 1930s a CN lounge car had a barbershop and radio and telephone service. Sleepers had tiled bathrooms with showers. Both CN and CP used velours upholstery and 400-year-old wood paneling imported from England.

Passenger cars at Whitbourne Station, headquarters of the Reid-Newfoundland Railway. Sir Robert G. Reid was a contractor who built Newfoundland's railway and operated it for twenty years.

In April 1955, both CN and CP introduced new transcontinental trains. CN's Super-continental consisted of cars from Canadian Car and Foundry and the Chicago-based Pullman Company. CN purchased 218 first-class coaches, 104 sleeping cars, 15 parlor cars, 14 diners and 6 dinettes — the largest Canadian order ever placed. CP received 173 stainless-steel cars from the Budd Company. The sleeping cars included 29 château-series cars, 42 manor-series cars and 18 park-series cars. The park-series cars, always coupled to the rear of the train, contain three double bedrooms, a drawing room, a lounge, a bar and an observation dome.

The VIA passenger service, which absorbed CN and CP equipment, has a fleet of 583 conventional passenger cars, 91 LRC cars and 70 self-propelled rail liners. The LRC (Light, Rapid and Comfortable) train is the latest addition, introduced to the Quebec-Windsor corridor in 1981. Its key feature, an automatic banking system for curves, does not function well. Although it is capable of 123 miles per hour, its maximum operating speed is 95. Rail officials have proposed that "dedicated" track (for exclusive use of passenger traffic) is necessary to improve speeds.

FREIGHT

In a single year, Canada's three major railways carry more than 200 million tons of freight.

Tonnages for the year 1983:

CN Rail	107.4 million tons
CP Rail	88.2 million tons
BC Rail	9.3 million tons

The leading commodities carried, in terms of tonnage, are grain and coal. In 1983 CN and CP moved a combined total of 43.2 million tons of grain and 28.9 million tons of coal.

Forest products, potash, sulphur and petrochemicals are also major freight commodities.

Vancouver and Thunder Bay are the country's busiest port outlets for major resources carried by rail. But the construction of new facilities for handling coal and grain at the port of Prince Rupert in northern British Columbia will transform the isolated CN terminal into an important Pacific resource outlet.

Freight rolling stock

Types of freight cars include boxcars, flatcars, hoppers, gondola cars, slurry cars, tank cars and tri-level automobile transporters, to name a few. CN owns 92,000 cars of all types; CP owns 62,000; BC Rail owns 10,000.

CN also claims to run the world's biggest rail barge, the **AquaTrain**, which operates year-round between Prince Rupert and Whittier, Alaska, a distance of 840 miles over open water. The trip takes four days each way. The AquaTrain has a capacity for 56 rail cars.

Canadian railways played a pioneering role in helping develop piggyback and container services during the 1960s. Both CN and CP have major inter-modal terminals.

INNOVATIONS

Robot locomotives: CP Rail introduced Canada's first remote-controlled mid-train diesels in regular service in 1967.

Unit trains are groups of identical, never-separated rail cars that continuously carry the same bulk commodity and constantly cycle between the same point of origin and destination. Both CN and CP use unit trains, principally for shipping coal across British Columbia to the Pacific coast, but also for moving sulphur, potash and oil. CP created Canada's first major unit train in 1967 when it shipped 3,600 tons of sulphuric acid through Ontario from Copper Cliff to Sarnia. CN introduced the world's first oil unit train in 1977, a rolling pipeline of 60 tank cars.

Technical research by CN has produced a locomotive computer that detects wheel slippage and automatically reduces power to the traction motors; self-steering freight cars that reduce wheel friction on curved sections of track; and the world's most advanced locomotive simulator.

Continuous welded rail (CWR), also known as "ribbon" rail, is installed in rail lengths of up to a quarter of a mile, mostly in the west, where track sustains heavy loads of coal freight. CN has approximately 8,000 miles of CWR; CP has about 4,000 miles. CN is also experimenting with concrete ties, which are used on about 1,000 miles of its system.

British Columbia Railway has been a major innovator. In its previous incarnation as the Pacific Great Eastern Railway, it became the first all-diesel line in North America, in the early 1950s. In 1983 it opened its branch line to the Tumbler Ridge coalfields, which became Canada's first electrified freight railway and only the third in the world to use a 50-kilovolt power supply. Motive power consists of 6,000-horsepower electric locomotives. British Columbia Railway also became the first North American railway to be thoroughly equipped with a microwave communications network. And it has developed a radio-controlled, computer-assisted method of directing and monitoring rail traffic with video-display units in locomotive cabs.

MISHAPS

The most serious accidents took place in the early days, before the advent of modern signaling and safety procedures.

A "wedge" snowplow being pushed by a Birkenhead locomotive between Lévis and Richmond, Quebec, in the winter of 1869. Manufactured in England, the Birkenheads were the first distinctively Canadian locomotives — their design was what a British manufacturer thought a Canadian locomotive ought to look like.

Canada's first railway collision took place on the Great Western Railway west of Chatham, Ontario, in 1854, when a train of ballast for building track collided with a passenger train and killed 47 people.

Canada's worst railway disaster occurred near the Quebec village of Beloeil just after 1:00 a.m. on June 29, 1864, when a passenger train flew off an open swing bridge spanning the Richelieu River. A tugboat was pulling a barge under the bridge when the train raced through the red signal lights and, whistle shrieking, plunged over the edge. The locomotive landed on the barge and the cars tumbled on top, one after the other. It was a special eleven-car train filled with 438 European immigrants, who had arrived on a German sailing ship just three days earlier. Most were bound for the American midwest. Ninety-seven passengers and two railway employees were killed. Two days later, the death toll reached an even hundred when a curious passenger who leaned out a passing train to view the wreckage was decapitated by a telegraph wire.

The engineer who sped over the open bridge was a novice unfamiliar with the route. He survived and was found negligent in a coroner's verdict. The coroner made recommendations that had a permanent impact on rail safety. Train crews were increased from four to five, and safety standards were stepped up. And the accident helped inspire a young American, George Westinghouse, to develop the concept of air brakes, first demonstrated in 1868.

From 1979 to 1983, there were an average of 312 derailments a year in Canada. The most serious derailment involving a freight train carrying a dangerous substance occurred on November 10, 1979, at 11:56 p.m., when 25 cars of a CP Rail train left the tracks in Mississauga, Ontario. Of the 25 cars, 19 carried hazardous goods; one was a tanker of lethal chlorine gas; it was punctured with a three-foot hole. Some 225,000 residents were evacuated and did not return to their homes for a week. There were no fatalities.

ROBBERIES

Canada's first train robbers were five unknown men disguised in white Ku Klux Klan robes who boarded the express car of the Great Western Railway between Toronto and Port Credit on November 13, 1874, and stole $45,000.

Canada's most celebrated train robber was an American —Bill Miner, a highwayman who served 34 years in United States jails before coming to British Columbia in 1904 under the name George Edwards. Known as "the Gentleman Bandit," he turned from robbing stagecoaches to robbing trains. On a September night in 1904, he and two masked accomplices stopped the CPR's Transcontinental Express by holding a gun to the engineer's head and stole $7,000 in cash and gold dust. In May 1906, he attempted a similar robbery but came away with a mailbag that contained almost nothing. The mounted police caught him later that year and he was sentenced to life imprisonment. The next year he escaped and fled to the United States, where he was jailed for a train robbery in Georgia, only to escape again. He was recaptured, escaped once more and was finally caught for the last time. He died in a Georgia prison hospital in 1913.

One of the original Royal Hudson locomotives, formerly part of the CPR fleet, now takes tourists on excursions between Vancouver and Squamish on the British Columbia Railway.